The Freethinkers' Pocket Directory to the Educational Universe

Written by
Roland Meighan

and edited by
James Meighan

Educational Heretics Press

Published 1995 by Educational Heretics Press
113 Arundel Drive, Bramcote Hills, Nottingham NG9 3FQ

British Cataloguing in Publication Data

Meighan, Roland

Freethinkers' Pocket Directory to the Educational Universe
I. Title II. Meighan, James
370

ISBN   0-9518022-6-7

Design, editing and production: James Meighan for Educational Heretics Press

Printed by Mastaprint, Sandiacre, Nottinghamshire

Contents

**Educational Heretics Press exists to question
the dogmas of education in general,
and schooling in particular.**

Introduction

Parents who look for an effective education for their children look for different things. Some in the UK will pay large sums of money to have their children go to the kind of boarding school that breaks-in young males like horses to 'toughen them up' for the 'real world'. Others look for the day-time equivalent.

Some parents look for an education based on natural learning principles, that begins, and hopefully ends, with happiness. Since state schools in the UK have been adopting more and more of the first view, the regressive approach, these parents have no option but to search, argue and organise to try to get what they seek elsewhere.

Like the vegetarian pioneers who wanted a more healthy diet, or the non-smokers who wanted to breathe nicotine-free air in public places, or the members of Charter 88 who want some real democracy in UK, these parents have no option but to do it themselves. It is not like this in other countries, especially the sixteen or so that lie above the UK in the league table that is based on the index of civilised nations. (UK has dropped about four places in the last ten years.)

In the quest for personalised education, one hundred parents a month in UK are currently opting out of schooling altogether to start home-based education. They are usually startled to find how successful this venture proves to be. Others seek small schools with a personalised curriculum. They are hard to find, but they do exist.

Elsewhere, alternative educational ideas appears to be a growth area. Some industrial concerns in the USA are now supporting alternative approaches with grants designed to:

"enable those entrepreneurs and risk-takers in education to break up the institutional gridlock that has stifled innovation and creativity"

in the words of Nabisco's chairman Louis V. Gerstner. The Nabisco scheme is to be known as "Next Century Schools" and has an initial £5.3 million given to it to: *"find bold ideas and see if they work"*.

Citibank is another commercial concern with a similar view. One of the first beneficiaries of Citibank's grants will be the Coalition of Essential Schools, based on the work of such people as Dr. Theodore Sizer at Brown University. This approach assumes that pupils are not vessels into which information is poured but active participants in deciding what and how they are to learn in the quest of learning how to think and use their minds.   The object is to train teachers in the alternative approach of being 'coaches' rather than authoritarian instructors.

Alternative educators in USA thus finds themselves in a situation where their ideas are changing from being seen as marginal to becoming of central interest. The schools, groups, families and individuals concerned are dedicated to providing the kind of flexible personalities and globally aware people needed to cope successfully with the society in which we live, as well as try to change it for the better.

This directory attempts to reach the parts other education directories do not reach. It had its origins in the irritation of those working with alternative ideas in education who found their work unrecognised in existing reference books. This omission is serious and not just a matter of hurt pride, for as Bertrand Russell pointed out, significant new ideas usually come from the non-conformists:

"Do not fear to be eccentric in opinion,
for every opinion now accepted as obvious was once eccentric."

The problem is, however, that alongside the fruitful ideas and critical analyses to be found in alternative thought and action, there is a considerable amount of speculative 'happy talk' and often harmless, but rather useless, self-indulgence. Alternative medicine shows the same pattern.   There are also a few counter-productive ideas too.   The contents have been selected with this problem in mind and the fifty or so entries represent the most promising horses in the alternatives educational stable, in the judgement of the editor, the writer and their advisory network.

Roland Meighan

Advisory Centre for Education (ACE)

ACE is an independent consumer organisation promoting wider openings for more children in education through increased openness and accountability in education. As well as this, ACE provides informed and unbiased advice for parents about how to involve parents in the education of their children and how, in association with schools, to obtain the most effective education for those children. ACE also informs parents about rights, requirements and responsibilities of all parties concerned regarding education.

Fundamental changes within the educational environment, now enshrined in governmental legislation, have theoretically given parents more of a role in their children's education, in terms of school selection and affecting the way in which their child(ren)'s school is run. Unfortunately, there is not much assistance provided to enable parents to utilise this 'power' to their best advantage, and ACE helps to fill this daunting void.

Since these changes (such as the provision for schools to opt out of Local Education Authority control and the imposition of a National Curriculum) have been explained in a sporadic fashion, parents often require assistance and support as they seek to use the chance to increase their involvement in the education of their offspring.

Information and advice is made available through various publications including handbooks, information sheets and a bi-monthly newsletter. ACE answers letters on educational matters and provides a confidential telephone help-line offering free advice. The advice given can include explanation and clarification of situations and procedures, legal advice, and if a question demands it, recommendation of other, more appropriate information sources.

Another function of ACE is campaigning on behalf of parents for their views to be considered with more credence by other members of the general public and, especially, politicians. Similarly, ACE lobbies for a shift of emphasis by school governors and staff towards taking children's educational experiences and opinions more seriously and adapting their practices/environments accordingly (children are, after all, the system's 'consumers').

ACE is a registered charity, and as such is reliant for finance upon grants, subscriptions, donations and income from publication sales.

The Authoritarian View of Education

Authoritarian education, in its various forms, has one person, or a small group of people, making and implementing the decisions about what to learn, when to learn, how to learn, how to assess learning, and the learning environment. These decisions are taken in course-planning committees and accreditation boards often before the learners are recruited as individuals or meet as a group.

Discipline is ... learning to obey the rules and instructions decided by an appointed individual or a senior management group.

Knowledge is ... essentially, information contained in the traditional subjects.

Learning is ... mostly, listening to subject experts and reading their books.

Teaching is ... usually, formal instruction by trained or approved adults.

Parents are ... expected, for the most part, to be spectators to the experts.

Resources are ... predominately, subject textbooks.

Location is ... a central place (school) where the experts (teachers) can easily be assembled together cheaply, with large groups of pupils.

Organisation is ... usually in classes formally arranged; the regimental nature of the activity often signalled by the wearing of uniforms.

Assessment is ... mostly, by tests of how well pupils can repeat the subjects.

Aims are ... essentially, to produce mini-academic subject experts, with those who fail in this enterprise, encouraged to gain the behaviours useful in manufacturing and commerce.

Power is ... in the hands of the appointed individual or a senior management team
or governors who believe that they have the right to impose their decisions on others.

(See *Autonomous View* and *Democratic View.*)

The Autonomous View of Education

In **autonomous education**, the decisions about learning are made by the individual learners. They manage their own learning programmes. They may seek advice or look for ideas about what to learn and how to learn it by research and consultation. They take responsibility for their own education.

Discipline is ... that form of discipline known as self-discipline.

Knowledge is ... essentially, the repertoire of learning and research skills needed to cope with expanding and changing databases.

Learning is ... mostly, self-directed activity and personal research to gain experience, information or particular skills.

Teaching is ... usually, self-teaching and the main purpose of a teacher other than yourself is to teach you how to teach yourself better.

Parents are ... expected, for the most part, to be part of the team supporting the learner's growth in learning skills and confidence.

Resources are ... predominately, first-hand experiences as the basis of personal research backed up by any other resources seen to be appropriate.

Location is ... anywhere that useful or interesting learning can take place.

Organisation is ... often in individual learning stations in institutional settings, but remains flexible to match the variety of learner-managed tasks.

Assessment is ... commonly, by self-assessment using any tests, devised by the learner or by others, that are seen to be appropriate to the situation.

Aims are ... essentially, to produce people with the confidence and skills to manage their own learning throughout their entire lives.

Power ... is seen as devolved to individuals who are seen as morally responsible for the exercise of their autonomy.

(See also *Authoritarian View* and *Democratic View*.)

Bullying

The problem with most discussions about bullying is that the root causes are overlooked. The focus is on the event of bullying and what to do about it, with an underlying assumption that the individual bully is an especially diseased person and the blame can therefore be heaped upon them. The question of where they learned this pattern of behaviour is avoided.

School, based on the current model of the compulsory day-prison, is itself a bully institution for it preaches forced attendance. Next it employs a bully curriculum - the compulsory National Curriculum. This is enforced by an increasingly imposed bully pedagogy of teacher-dominated formal teaching. The hidden curriculum of this package is that adults get their way by bullying children. Even if only a few of the children apply this idea immediately to become bullies in the playground, the long term message turns up when other children become teachers in the bully tradition or parents adopting the 'it's for your own good' version of child upbringing.

Until we replace this morbid model with a new model of the voluntary attendance, 'invitational' school operating within a flexible education system, bullying will continue to be 'taught'.

Alice Miller observes that every persecutor was once a victim. Every bully was once bullied. The behaviour has to be learned. The bully institution of school does not operate in a vacuum, however. As Jerry Mintz reports from the USA:

> "American kids like watching violence on TV and in the movies because violence is being done to them, both at school and at home. It builds up a tremendous amount of anger ... The problem is not violence on TV. That's a symptom ... The real problem is the violence of anti-life, unaffectionate, and punitive homes, and disempowering, deadening compulsory schooling, all presented with an uncomprehending smile."

Of course, the symptoms have to be dealt with. Schools need to devise an anti-bullying policy. But preventing the disease starting in the first place will require rethinking the basic model of schooling, the curriculum and the act of teaching itself.

The Children's Legal Centre (CLC)

An independent national charity, the Children's Legal Centre opened in 1981, and is funded by grants, donations and publication sales. It is concerned with getting young people, including children, involved with the legal decisions which affect their futures. The CLC represents young people wherever decisions affecting them are made - courts, chambers of government, and any other meetings of influential groups.

Information, counselling and advice are provided by telephone and letter; conferences and courses are organised and research projects initiated and carried out. The CLC is constantly checking statements, announcements and events which affect young peoples' legal position; responding as appropriate.

Further information, summaries, legal explanation and clarification are provided by the Centre's publications. The most regular of these is the subscription-only bulletin "Childright". Other publications are by the nature of information sheets, reports, guides, books of various lengths on a range of subjects including corporal punishment, attending court, the environment and teenagers' eligibility for benefits.

The services provided by the CLC are used by young people, parents and anyone working with young people - individuals or groups - who need to know how the law in England and Wales affects them and their associated young people. Enquiries may not be limited to an initial question, but might need to be pursued further, for example to another advisory body, local MP, court, or to seek further information through research.

By the above means, the Children's Legal Centre tries to galvanise young people into being a much better-informed group in society; aware of decisions affecting them and able to influence policy-making wherever possible. In situations where young people are unable to represent themselves and their views, the Children's Legal Centre will undertake that task on a protective basis. This situation might occur, for example, if very young or handicapped children were involved.

The overall purpose of the Children's Legal Centre can be summarised as strengthening the position of the youth of England and Wales by thorough and unbiased provision and representation of information and advice to increase their independence and equality.

City As School (CAS)

Established in 1972 in New York, City As School was a response to the high dropout rate of the city's other high schools. Originators Fred Koury and Richard Safran wanted to provide a school with the flexibility to meet the individual needs of its pupils far more closely than the curricula of existing schools evidently did.

A choice of around 2500 'Learning Experiences' is on offer. Each has its own curriculum and a duration of 25 to 32 hours per week for nine weeks. The nine week time-span is considered to be long enough to be meaningful, without becoming torturous if a student encounters problems. The curriculum is agreed upon by the students in conjunction with a resource co-ordinator from the CAS. When the nine week 'mini-apprenticeship' concludes, the observations and reactions of both the curriculum provider and the student are sought.

The variety of 'Learning Experiences' is not just denoted by subject matter. Some units can be arranged to take place at un-school-like hours, such as at weekends or evenings, which can be useful if a separate interest is to be accommodated, such as art or sport courses.

By its nature, the City As School is dependant upon what the city offers as resources and facilities. Consequently, basic reading, writing and mathematics courses for the age groups involved can be hard to find. The CAS responds by itself putting these courses, in its own classrooms.

The method of meeting any needs still not met is to set up a project for the student, requiring use of the resources of the CAS as well as the city. Books, video and audio cassettes are available, as well as people. The nine week module duration still applies. Students can join the CAS at any time of the year, due to the relatively short nature of the 'Learning Experiences', compared with the common year-long school curriculum.

The flexibility of City As School, coupled with the involvement of students in the curriculum arrangement, results in a feeling for the students that they are being respected and treated as maturing adults, capable of making their own decisions and managing their own time profitably, when given the opportunity.

Community Education

The Community Education Association's manifesto declares that community education:

- is a concept of education being a life-long learning process concerned with identifying and meeting the needs of individuals and their communities;

- enables people to take greater control of their own learning and to participate fully in the making of decisions which affect them and communities of which they are part;

- encourages individuals and groups to take personal and collective action and responsibility leading to a fully active society in which common effort is made to improve everyone's quality of life.

Harry Reé, in his biography of Henry Morris, writes:

"Henry Morris started Community Education. He did this in two ways. First he sketched out a new philosophy of education, and then basing his plans on that philosophy, he persuaded the Cambridgeshire County Council to build a series of Village Colleges, which were the prototype for the Community Schools which are to be found all over the country today."

The ten Village Colleges of Cambridgeshire were to be located in market towns and they would serve everyone by bringing together in one location the schools, social services, medical services, county library, careers office, agricultural education, further education, the Workers' Educational Association, the youth services, playing fields and sports facilities. The sharing of these facilities would mean that the complex served as a community centre for the neighbourhood. The antithesis of community education would appear to be the English Public School. Hitler may have admired them as a model institution for producing the leaders of the Fatherland; Morris did not:

"The case against them is moral. The English nation has been riven into two nations, not on any principle based on virtue or intelligence but on money."

Compulsory Schooling Disease?

After twenty-five years as a modern languages teacher, Chris Shute, in his first book, *Compulsory Schooling Disease*, presents his misgivings about schooling:

"I agreed to write this book because, after twenty-five years of school-teaching, I became convinced that I was engaged in a form of microcosmic fascism. I intend to show in this book that schooling is, indeed, an activity which has aspects in common with fascism. That is not to say that teachers mean it to be so, or that they are conscious of the evil in which they are involved. Even fascism in its early phases attracted some reasonable, high-minded people who believed that the world could be changed for the better merely by the use of a little force and rigour in the right place."

"Perhaps their (my fellow teachers) true motivation was summed up for me by a lady colleague of mine some years ago. I had been talking to her about the grey, strained expressions I saw on the faces of my pupils as they went about the school. I suggested that it might be something to do with their feeling that they were not being educated so much as sentenced to hard labour for the crime of being children. She thought for a moment, and said in a grim voice: 'I went through it. I see no reason why my child should escape.'"

"I cannot bring myself to see education as she (my colleague) saw it, a life-long campaign against spontaneity, liveliness, and the natural energy of youth. Neither can I accept that the anger and frustration I saw in those children, which I now recognise as the same anger that slaves and occupied people feel, serves any good purpose in education."

"Home-based education or home-schooling is not discussed. This is not because I do not take it seriously as a method of educating children. In fact, I believe it is currently the best way to educate most children. But I hope that one day soon it will be possible for children to use schools as they should be used, as places where any person who happens to need help with their studies can go and receive it. Until that time, I must confine myself to commenting on schools as they are now, and challenging us to consider whether their regime contributes to enslaving the minds of children rather than setting them free."

Shute concludes that compulsory schooling is the *cause* of many social problems it claims to be trying to cure.

Computers and Dyslexia

Iris Harrison writes that, having watched Geoff, her husband, compose his first ever letter by using DragonDictate, and with such ease, she is now aware that at long last we have the tool to empower those with dyslexia or any similar kind of condition. With voice input software of this kind, anyone can become their own word processing expert and maximise their literacy skills at the same time. It enables individuals to help themselves.

The case of Jessica Bunzi, proprietor of Clandestine Software, illustrates the same point, when she writes: *"I have disability in my right hand and dyslexia. My main application for speech recognition is writing training courses and installation notes using WordPerfect 5.1 and a Compaq 486C. Speech recognition has opened up the world of written English. I am now able to use words that I cannot spell and can continue working regardless of my physical condition. I am now one hundred per cent productive. I now have extended periods of being able to function normally, mainly due to the relief that the speech recognition has given my hand."*

Dr. Les Kingham is Systems Development Manager of Aptech Ltd. and describes the development of this technology:

"Voice recognition allows computers to be controlled by simply speaking into a microphone. The technology has improved greatly in the last few years. ... Now we have systems that adapt and learn to recognise the operator's voice as he or she speaks. These recognisers have vocabularies of up to 30,000 words ... We at Aptech have supplied many of these 'listening word processor' systems to people with physical disabilities, enabling them to write documents even though they cannot type. Many have gone on to gain employment or to further or higher education."

Les goes on to sound a note of caution. Some spelling is needed to help train the voice recogniser. There are ways to reduce this problem, in particular by having a helper close by to make any necessary corrections during the first few hours with the system. But for perfectionists, 100% accuracy is unlikely to be achieved by everyone, although 80-90% can be expected in most cases. Nevertheless, from nil written competence to writing with 80% accuracy is still a huge leap forward! It is not the solution for *every* dyslexic person, but few who try it will be disappointed.

Curriculum Alternatives

The Imposed Subjects Curriculum relies heavily on the idea that one or more adults in power know what it is best for children to know, think and do. The National Curriculum of the USSR had as its central aim the production of young communists with subjects and contents chosen accordingly, whereas the aim in Hitler's Germany was to produce young fascists and required a different set of contents. The UK National Curriculum selects subjects to produce people who 'know their place' (official quote) in a capitalist social class order.

The Imposed Interpretative Curriculum also assumes that some adults know best what children should learn. Some involvement of the learners is attempted, however, by encouraging a dialogue between the learners and the teacher. This approach requires a more flexible view of knowledge, learning through exploring connected themes. It has been called the child-centred approach, but *child-referenced* is more apt since some reference is made to the children's world.

Imposed Confidence-Building Curriculum gives top priority to the skills of learning themselves. In this approach to the curriculum, the confidence to learn and re-learn and the skills of finding or creating information, organising, sifting and evaluating findings can be practised on a variety of topics so that the need for a set agenda is avoided. Fragmentation is not seen as a critical problem since the learners are acquiring the tools to fill gaps as and when necessary and the approach is seen as self-correcting in this respect.

The Consultative Curriculum is initially based on an imposed programme. This may be one of the three types outlined above or some combination of them since they do not necessarily exist in isolation. Into this imposed curriculum are built regular opportunities for the learners to be consulted about the programme. Their feedback may result in modifications to the curriculum.

The Negotiated Curriculum. Here, the degree of power-sharing increases. What emerges is an agreed contract with individuals and sometimes groups as to the nature of the course of study to be undertaken. The negotiation is an attempt to link the concerns and consciousness of the learners with the world of systematic knowledge and the experience of the adult tutor.

The Democratic Curriculum. When a group of learners design, implement and review their own curriculum, starting out with a blank piece of paper, power sharing has reached the point of democratic practice. The learners take on the roles of researchers and explorers; the teachers are facilitators and fixers. The course begins in a consultative mode for the teacher initiates the debate of the options. The group then decides whether to switch to the democratic mode.

Dame Catherine's School

There has been a school at Ticknall, south Derbyshire, since 1744. Dame Catherine Harpur established a trust to provide a school for children of the local area. Later it was taken over by the Local Education Authority who closed it in 1987 because it was seen as too small.

The local parents immediately re-opened it as a non-fee-paying parent-teacher co-operative venture for 5 to 16 year-olds and it now has about 50 children enrolled as students. Money is raised by the parents, children, teachers and friends of the school. A major source of funds is the Catherine Wheel gift shop run by the parents. Other money comes from covenants and donations and also from Educational Trusts.

The approach to education that has been developed in the school by the parents and teachers stresses small groups, close parental involvement in the organisation and some teaching support, and a curriculum adapted to suit individual needs. A tutorial system is the basis of the curriculum. Assignments are agreed with the teacher for the week and each child keeps a log of work showing what has been completed. The general aim is to enable children to develop their skills of learning how to learn, rather than diminishing them into learning how to be taught. The emphasis is on individualised education, or learner-managed learning, supported and coached by sensitive adults.

The parents persuaded an experienced head teacher Philip Toogood, who was Co-ordinator of the Human Scale Education Movement at the time, to run the school on human scale lines. The philosophy was based on the development of the whole person, body, mind and spirit, in a family-like atmosphere with teachers who are both friends and mentors and parents who are active partners in their children's education. Parents take the children swimming, to the library, the gym, help in the classroom, clean the school, repair and maintain the building, as well as raising the money. Because they are such a part of school life, they have their own pigeonholes in the lobby for ease of communication.

Education Now has been associated with the school from the start and has been a ready and indispensable source of help, advice and support. This was noted as an important factor in the school's success by HMI during their recent inspection which resulted in a favourable report on the school.

The Democratic View of Education

In **democratic education**, the learners as a group have the power to make some, most, or even all of the key decisions, since power is shared and not appropriated in advance by a minority of one or more. Ironically, in many 'democratic' countries, such educational practices are rare and often meet with sustained, hostile and irrational opposition.

Discipline is ... democratic discipline by working co-operatively to agreed and negotiated rules and principles.

Knowledge is ... essentially the skills and information needed by the group to maintain, develop, and sometimes, regenerate its co-operative culture.

Learning is ... activity agreed by the group to gain experience, information or particular skills working either together or delegated to individuals.

Teaching is ... any activity, including authoritarian forms of instruction, that the group judges will lead to effective learning.

Parents are ... expected, for the most part, to be part of the resources available.

Resources are ... anything the group sees as appropriate to the group's research and learning including people, places and experiences.

Location is ... anywhere that the learning group can meet to pursue learning.

Organisation is......commonly in group settings where democratic dialogue and co-operative learning can take place.

Assessment is......... by any form of assessment using any tests, devised by the learners or by others, that are seen to be appropriate to the situation.

Aims are.....essentially, to produce people with the confidence and skills to manage their own life-long learning within a democratic culture.

Power is......shared by the individuals in the group who are seen as morally responsible both individually and collectively for the exercise of it.

(See *Authoritarian View* and *Autonomous View*.)

John Dewey

The curiculum approach advocated by Dewey was **interactionist**, for he wrote: *"It is continuous reconstruction, moving from the child's present experience out into that represented by the organised bodies of knowledge."*
There were two errors Dewey identified and set out to avoid in his work on education. The first error stressed a curriculum centred on the experience of children, the second a curriculum based on the experience accumulated in the adult world in the form of subjects. This division into two opposed curriculum camps he saw as absurd. Those who proposed leaving children to their own unguided devices were as absurd as those who proposed that children should be taught in a totalitarian way by a formal succession of adult-dictated directions. Dewey sought the middle way of **interaction** between the two.

There was another aspect of schooling that he saw as an error. It was the gap that had developed between schools and the world of work. Dewey proposed that there should be a permanent and **organic connection between schools and business life.** The school was not seen as preparing children for any particular business but developing general work experience and understandings. Thus his experimental school centred the curriculum around practical 'occupations' such as textiles, cooking and construction with tools. He was also in favour of what would now be called a **value-added principle** that children who come to school with all the experience they have got outside the school should leave it at the end of the day with something that is additional and useful which can be of immediate use in everyday life.

Dewey saw **teachers as learning coaches** rather than mere instructors. In one example he takes the impulse of children to use pencil and paper:

> *"If you simply indulge this impulse by letting the child go on indefinitely, there is no growth that is more than accidental. But let the child first express the impulse, and then through criticism, question, and suggestion bring him to consciousness of what he has done, and what he needs to do, and the result is quite different."*

It was fundamental that such teachers were good organisers. Organisation he defined as nothing more and nothing less than getting things into connection with one another, so that they work easily, flexibly and fully.

Discipline: three kinds of discipline and various kinds of error

People sometimes think that discipline is the simple problem of adults making children behave to instructions. This is only one kind of discipline - the authoritarian. Three kinds can be identified. They are:

1. **Authoritarian** - where order is based on rules imposed by adults. Power resides in an individual or group of leaders.
2. **Autonomous** - where order is based on self-discipline and self-imposed rational rules. Power resides with the individual.
3. **Democratic** - where order is based on rules agreed after rational discussion, i.e. based on evidence, human rights values and the logic of consequences. Power is shared amongst the people in the situation.

There has been a centuries-old debate about which of these three is the best system of discipline. It is now a sterile debate. The complexities of modern life are such that all three types of discipline have a place to play in the scheme of things. Sometimes we need to follow instructions or take on leadership roles thus following the authoritarian approach. In an aeroplane, debating who should fly the aircraft and the rules of flying is not the appropriate form of discipline that matches the situation. In a car, the driver needs autonomous discipline and to make the decisions about driving the car without the confusions of being over-ruled by an authoritarian, or advised by a committee of back-seat drivers.

In many other situations, 'several heads are likely to be better than one' in deciding the rules to be adopted, based on the evidence and the rights of all involved. Power-sharing, although time-consuming, is then likely to lead to better, fairer, and agreed decisions with co-operative system of order.

It follows that there are three types of error as regards discipline. One, the current error of most UK schooling, is to select the authoritarian as the predominant approach. The second, the error of some radical thinkers, is to make the autonomous the One Right Way. The third error from another radical tradition, is to make the democratic the exclusive approach. All these One Right Way approaches fail to match the need for young people to learn what most of their elders have clearly failed to learn, that is how to be competent in the logistics and practice of all three types of discipline, and to select them appropriately.

Education Now

This group is a forum in which people with differing, diverse and undogmatic views can develop dialogue about alternatives to existing dominant and compulsory forms of education. It aims to stimulate and inform educational debate through conferences, courses, consultancy, research and publishing. Its **Statement of Purpose** declares that **EDUCATION NOW** thinks that the word *education* has come to be misunderstood. Many people assume that it means 'what teachers do with children in school' and nothing else. **EDUCATION NOW** challenges that view. Its understanding of *education* is much wider, encompassing the many beneficial experiences which take place outside schools and colleges and which lead to valuable learning. It opposes those elements in the present system which promote uniformity, dependency, and, for many, a lasting sense of failure.

The vision of **EDUCATION NOW** includes:
1. a focus on the uniqueness of individuals, of their learning experiences and of their many and varied learning styles;
2. support of education in human scale settings including home-based education, small schools, mini-schools, and schools-within-schools, flexischooling and flexi-colleges;
3. recognition that learners themselves have the ability to make both rational and intuitive choices about their education;
4. advocacy of co-operative and democratic organisation of places of learning;
5. belief in the need to share national resources so that everyone has a real choice in education;
6. acceptance of Einstein's proposal that *imagination is more important than knowledge* in our modern and constantly changing world;
7. adoption of the Universal Declaration of Human Rights in general and the European Convention for the Protection of Human Rights and Fundamental Freedoms in particular.

EDUCATION NOW maintains that people learn best:
- when they are self-motivated
- when they take responsibility for their own lives and learning
- when they feel comfortable in their surroundings
- when teachers and learners value, trust, respect and listen to each other
- when education is seen as a life-long process.

EDUCATION NOW rejects those forms of education which cause learners to feel frightened, bored and frustrated, thus harming them and reducing their capacity for learning. It works to celebrate and develop constructive alternatives to such forms within, alongside and outside them.

Flexi-schooling

Flexi-schooling is a new blueprint for education derived from the notion that the conventional rigid model of schooling is no longer an adequate vehicle for the development of young people. The idea was developed in discussions between John Holt and Roland Meighan in 1984 during Holt's last visit to England, and not long before his death from cancer. The key idea is that:

"rigid systems produce rigid people, flexible systems produce flexible people."

Flexi-schooling developed, at first, as a more open way of viewing the partnership of home, school and community. Some parents do not want to consign their children totally to an educational institution which claims to do the whole job of educating their children for them. Nor do they want to do all of it themselves in a home-based education programme, although many are forced to do so as best option open to them. What they seek is a way of having the best of both worlds in the interests of serving their children's needs in a world of rapid change.

Flexi-schooling, even in its first version as **flexi-time**, (see entry on flexi-time) could be seen to be questioning the basic assumptions of compulsory schooling in Britain in the 1990s:

1. **There does not have to be a single location for education.** There can be several, including schools, homes, work-places, museums and libraries.
2. **Parents are seen as having an active educational role** in co-operation and partnership with schools and capable of building on their astonishing achievements of helping their children learn to talk, walk and develop in the first five years of life.
3. **Children can learn many things without a teacher being present.** After all, they managed to learn their mother tongue this way.
4. **Teaching is not synonymous with instructing.** 'Learning Coach' activities, such as helping them locate resources to further their own research, are types of teaching. Thus, facilitating learning is a teaching act as well as 'full frontal' instruction.
5. **Resources available at home can be utilized in educational programmes.** These include the ubiquitous T.V. and radio, as well as cassette recorders, video recorders, and home computers.
6. **The uniqueness of individuals can be respected.** Different learning styles can be accommodated in a more flexible system.

In later expanded versions, flexi-schooling is seen as a much more flexible approach to education **in all its dimensions**, and it raises more questions still. For example, could the curriculum become a negotiated experience more than an imposed one? Could there be choice from the variety of types of curriculum available? In general, it offers the prospect of diversifying, starting from the rigid school system, without losing any positive features that can be identified.

Although flexi-schooling sounds futuristic, a central finding is that some of the key components are already available and operational in different schools, homes and community locations, and in various countries. It is an attempt to see how a new model of schooling can be generated out of the old to respond to the needs of a society in the throes of a communications revolution. We have a changing world. Its technologies and its cultures continue to change and become more complicated. Knowledge continues to grow and existing knowledge is shown to be partial and sometimes in error. Rigid people cannot cope: flexible people have a better chance of coping.

Behaviour in the modern world is also complex. Sometimes we need **authoritarian** behaviour, i.e. the types of responses and people who know when it makes sense to take orders or give them. At other times we need the self-managing skills of **autonomous** behaviour, and at other times the co-operative skills of **democratic** behaviour. The world is multi-dimensional. An adequate education means helping people to grow to match it. Our present school system is, for the most part, uni-dimensional by offering predominantly authoritarian experiences.

John Holt has a proposal about how schools could be **invitational** rather than based on conscription. It goes like this:

"Why not make schools into places where children would be allowed, encouraged, and, when they asked, helped to make sense of the world around them in ways that interested them?"

In flexi-schooling, it is proposed that we should rename such places as **learning resource centres** to avoid confusion with the 'day-prison', compulsory attendance, adult-imposed curriculum model of a school.

Flexi-time

For some parents and their children the best arrangement for learning is for part of the time to be at home, and for part of the time to be at school. Some flexi-time arrangements are relatively easy to achieve. These are when **large blocks of time** are spent either at school or at home:

1. The whole of the primary years are devoted to home-based education, then the secondary years given over to school.
2. The reverse pattern, primary phase in school, secondary phase home-based.
3. Whole years in school, or college, and whole years home-based, as and when seen to be appropriate.
4. In the same way, whole terms are spent either in school or home-based.

The most **difficult** arrangement appears to be that of a **flexible week** with two or three days in school and two or three days home-based. This is commonplace in nursery schools in the UK and also later in colleges at the further education phase where flexi-study programmes are made available, and also in some cases in higher education.

The position in law in the UK is that there are two *absolute* rights in education, either to educate at home or to use a school. Flexi-time is a *relative* right so that a school or Local Education Authority can arrange this, but if permission is refused, no reason has to be given. So, each arrangement has to be negotiated afresh, and parents have patiently to explain that it **is** permissible and that plenty of people **have** done it and are doing it, and that it **does** work very well if the will and the vision are there.

Strangely enough, it immediately becomes possible if parents will allow their child to be labelled odd and accept a 'school phobic' label or 'school refuser' description or some other categorisation.

In the USA flexible week arrangements are called Independent Study Programmes or ISPs and are becoming more common. A specially trained member of staff negotiates the timetable with the families concerned.

At first, the idea of flexi-time was described as flexi-schooling in the UK, but the latter notion grew in scope to cover much more than just part-time schooling, so the terms now need to be more carefully distinguished.

(See entry on *Flexi-schooling*.)

Free Schools

Thirteen free schools were set up in England in the 1970s. One by one they failed due mainly to the problems of financing. Sometimes the financial problems were aggravated by the problems of making the philosophy of freedom work with unco-operative children who had been too severely damaged by the authoritarian regimes of their past. Several school were forced to made deals with Local Education Authorities to take in their most difficult children in return for grants, in order to survive financially.

The schools were an attempt to pioneer a radically different kind of schooling for inner-city children. Children were free to learn what they wanted to learn, so long as it did not interfere with anyone else. The schools were all independent schools in an attempt to be free of the bureaucracy experienced by state schools.

Freedom was not seen as the mere absence of restraints, but more positively as the freedom to make significant choices amongst various activities and alternatives. Without valid options, freedom was seen as rather meaningless. To achieve this, the restraints on children needed to be at a minimum. Different schools devised different operational definitions of minimum restraints.

The idea of using some form of democracy as the main organisational device was common to all the schools. Here too, the definitions used varied and sometimes simplistic notions of democracy as 'one person one vote' were adopted and were then be found to be wanting. More sophisticated and successful versions of democracy did not always emerge from this experience. The longest-surviving example was the White Lion Street Free School, discussed by Nigel Wright in his book *Free School* (Libertarian Education 1989).

Wright suggests that the Free Schools underestimated the power of external forces and therefore over-estimated what could be achieved in the short term. A mundane example was that of food. The lunches prepared in the school were seen as an opportunity to introduce more nutritional and healthier eating habits. The outside world had already set up the eating habits of greasy chips, fish fingers, sugar-treated baked beans and the like. Many children refused to try unfamiliar food or accept the arguments about health, so no changes occurred, only increased tensions. There was, in Wright's view, too much wishful thinking and not enough hard thinking about the theory and practice of freedom.

Paulo Freire

Freire initiated a programme in which literacy training and political awareness discussions were intertwined. His pedagogy is built on three fundamental ideas, consciousness, dialogue and praxis. **Consciousness** implied becoming aware, not just 'knowing about', but a personal and critical awareness of the social nature of existential problems. Continuous **dialogue** amongst the participants deepened and developed this awareness through reflection and articulation into action. **Praxis** meant that the new knowledge, i.e. raised consciousness, should lead to actions to change the world for the better, not just to endure it. The message of the 'pedagogy of the oppressed' was that people as they transform themselves begin the transformation of the world. Hitler observed that it was fortunate for those in power that the people were unable to think. Freire reversed the equation: people who do learn to think, in the process of becoming literate, can begin to change the world.

The role of the teacher was redefined. The instructor model was rejected in favour of the role of an agent of reflection whose task was to support the learning process of the student. The instructor model depended on the **banking concept of knowledge:**

"It follows logically from the banking notion of consciousness that the educator's role is to regulate the way the world 'enters into' the students. His task is to organise a process which already happens spontaneously, to 'fill' the students by making deposits of information which he considers constitute true knowledge. And since men 'receive' the world as passive entities, education should make them more passive still, and adapt them to the world. The educated man is the adapted man, because he is more 'fit' for the world. Translated into practice, this concept is well suited to the purpose of the oppressors, whose tranquillity rests on how well men fit the world the oppressors have created, and how little they question it. "

He rejected the 'banking concept' of knowledge that dominated conventional schooling, the mere transfer of blocks of information from teacher to learner as if these were bank deposits to be withdrawn at a later date. Freire developed an adult literacy scheme in one of the poorest parts of the world where starvation, the lack of medical care, employment and education were commonplace. His work was seen as a threat to those who came to power, and in 1964 he was expelled to Chile. He has since worked in USA (at Harvard), Geneva, Africa and elsewhere.

Friedrich Froebel

Two ideas are usually associated with the name of Froebel, the Kindergarten and the value of play in education. He was German born (1782) and he later worked in Switzerland. He held that education was concerned with three inter-related aspects of experience, and these were activity, emotions and intellect. Thus, all children learn by being active and this activity produces emotional responses as well as mental responses. The three aspects which can be analysed apart, are in practical life indivisible or inter-active. Education, he proposed, should be:

> "... lively, must be relevant to their lives, and must not be empty words, dead ideas nor a mere game of the intellect."

To make education meaningful, we need to start with the environment, our relationship with nature and with the people around us. This will lead us into reflective thinking, and since Froebel was religious, into a religious interpretation of living. Motivation starts with the child, but specifically with what a child can already do well:

> "To awaken the pupil's urge for learning by concentrating on what he can do well, is the highest and first goal of the education of the people and especially the poor. This drive can easily be awakened in a free and tolerant situation, for every human being ultimately wants to be completely what his inclination and ability allows him to be."

Froebel had a place in his approach for reflective imitation, rather than thoughtless copying, and saw it as the first step towards creativity. He thought that it was not possible to teach creativity, but it was possible to arrange situations which developed lateral thinking. Play was important in developing such thinking, but guided play was more important than unguided:

> "Play must therefore not be left to chance, for it is through play that the child learns and learns eagerly and with enjoyment. Time must be allocated to play just as much as to lessons and activities. Because it is so important it does not only need the careful guidance of the teacher, but may have to be initiated by him."

For Froebel, a good school was like a good home and had similar aims, stressing:
satisfaction, joy, unity, mutual helpfulness, trust and co-operation.

Paul Goodman

The writings of Paul Goodman were at first ignored, then ridiculed, but eventually acclaimed as visionary. The book *Growing Up Absurd* became a best-seller and *Compulsory Miseducation* set in motion a fierce debate about the effects of schooling. He was born in New York in 1911 and died in 1972.

Schooling, he said, was a **mass superstition:** the superstition that education can only be achieved in an institution like a school. He stated that subjecting young people to institutionalised learning tends to stunt and distort their natural intellectual development and finally turns out regimented, competitive citizens likely to aggravate our current social ills. It is **compulsory miseducation.** Instead, we should encourage the natural learning patterns of family and community, and promote the sort of learning relationships fostered in the best master-apprentice traditions. School, as currently organised, he saw as entirely artificial whereas education was a natural experience. Some critics said that schools are geared to middle-class values. He disagreed, saying that schools represented no positive human values, but adjustment to a mechanical system:

> "It is in the schools and from the mass media, rather than at home or from their friends, that the mass of our citizens in all classes learn that life is inevitably graded; that it is best to toe the mark and shut up; that there is no place for spontaneity, open sexuality, free spirit."

The schools were likely to continue despite their miseducation and their obsolescence because of a series of vested interests:
1. One was that of employment, so that it went on for its own sake keeping millions of people busy and wasting wealth. It was a gigantic market for textbook publishers, building contractors and university graduates.
2. Another was the baby-sitting and teenager-containing functions. With the breakdown of the old-style extended family, schoolteachers were in the early years mother substitutes and in the later stages, police substitutes.
3. Third was the selection and training function for industry where a system provided at public expense saved industry and commerce the trouble of providing effective apprenticeship schemes.

In Goodman's view the aim of education must be to get everyone out of their small divisive social worlds of class and nation into the one humanity.

As regards democracy, he claimed that the American tradition was that citizens were **society-makers,** not just participating in or adjusting to society. But, currently citizens felt powerless: they had lost the content of democracy and were left only with the trappings.

Green Education and Green Teacher

Green Teacher is a publication devoted to providing support and suggestions for those intent on making their education methods more environmentally aware. Teachers are the most obvious target, but any educators - professional or otherwise - may find it of use, as well as teacher-trainers, school governors and other curriculum-devisors.

It has been run from a base at the Centre for Alternative Technology in Powys, Wales, since its first edition in October 1986 under the editorship of Damian Randle, with some editions being taken over partially or totally by interested groups or individuals. Green Teacher is run by a co-operative on a non-profit making basis.

Green Teacher stresses its international interests; it has a related magazine in Canada and does not concentrate solely on British educational issues. Around ten per cent of Green Teacher copies are sent abroad.

Issues in Green Education published by Education Now, is a collection of key articles taken from The Green Teacher. The book recognises that the greening of education has made a start and that 'environmental education' has come a long way in a short time. But more needs to be done if the questions of deep ecology and social ecology are to be answered. Questions raised include: 'Is green education the same as holistic education?' A manifesto for education for the twenty-first century, based on holistic principles, is offered for review. Another question raised is whether 'green' thinking has paid too little attention to the concerns and insights of their 'red' radical predecessors.

Issues in Green Education and The Green Teacher journal itself, offer no ready-made solutions, but try to stimulate further debate, both practical and philosophical. The practical approach is exemplified in items such as the Green School Survey which contains twenty-five questions that teachers, students, parents can ask about their school in attempting an audit of their environmental values in practice. This appeared in Green Teacher number 22 and is reprinted in the book.

Damian Randle has written a guide, *Teaching Green: a parent's guide to education for life on earth* which is useful in schools or in an home-based education context. It opens up debate about the ecological, resources, energy, social/political and world relations crises that we face in the modern world.

The Hidden Curriculum

The hidden curriculum refers to an **unwritten curriculum** that carries the long-term, permanent messages of compulsory mass schooling when the authoritarian model is adopted as the dominant organisational approach. These messages include the following:

> Passive acceptance is preferable to active criticism,
> Discovering knowledge is not a task for pupils,
> Recall and regurgitation are the highest for.ł.s of intellectual
>   achievement suitable for pupils,
> The voice of authority is to be automatically obeyed,
> The feelings of pupils are irrelevant,
> Education consists of memorising the provided Right Answers,
> Competition is more important than co-operation,
> Helping others always gives way to getting on oneself,
> Writing and reading are more important than talking and thinking,
> Men are more important than women,
> Dogma is more desirable than doubt.

Few teachers set out to teach these by design, except perhaps some teachers of religion in the case of the last message, that dogma is more desirable than doubt. The messages of the hidden curriculum are conveyed gradually and persistently by the apparatus of an institution that is based on compulsion and dominated by an authoritarian outlook. These messages are even more severe under the principles of regressive schooling.

Another source of the hidden curriculum is the **peer group.** Children are compelled to spent 15,000 hours minimum in the forced company of their peers. There is an opportunity cost. They lose the chance to mix with adults out and about in society, and gradually become enrolled and imprisoned in the youth culture instead. The price to be paid varies from an ageist outlook addiction, to clothes-fashion addiction, to pop music addiction, to smoking addiction, to drug addiction, to minor and sometimes major crime. Families who decide to opt out for home-based education frequently refer to the 'tyranny of the peer group' as one of the key reasons for their decision.

High/Scope Perry Pre-school Project

The curriculum developed at the High/Scope Perry Pre-School Project in Ypsilanti, Michigan, is based on active, child-initiated learning experiences. Children first decide and plan what they intend to do, then carry out their plans and finally reflect on what they have achieved. A wide range of materials and equipment is arranged on shelves accessible to the children, who have freedom to select what is most appropriate for their purposes. The approach can be applied in either school or home-based situations. Combining choice with routine, it is claimed, is particularly valuable for children with learning difficulties.

Plan: The early efforts in planning usually involve the child talking with an adult. Lucy, aged three, has the support of a pre-school worker as she talks about her intention to paint a picture. Together they consider what is to be painted, which paper to select, the type of paints to be used, where to paint... Older children engage in more challenging experiences and show greater confidence and independence. Tom, aged six, plans to make a model boat. He first talks through his ideas with his teacher and then draws up a plan of the boat, decides on the materials and tools, considers its size, and purpose.

Do: The implementation of the planning involves perseverance to see it through, perhaps modification of initial ideas, as well as the use of a range of skills and the ownership of subsequent knowledge.

Review: When children have completed their task they reflect on their achievements. For very young children this may mean talking with an adult about what they have been doing, but as they gain further experience they are encouraged to evaluate and justify their actions, not only to an adult but also to a small group of their peers who participate in the review process.

Outcomes of active, child-initiated learning experiences include:
- a sense of personal control and skills in learner-managed learning
- first-hand experiences encourage problem solving, reasoning, discovery
- the acquisition of key concepts and a range of skills, including language skills
- learning how to learn rather than learning how to be taught
- the development of traits important for lifelong learning, such as: confidence, curiosity, initiative, independence, responsibility, divergent thinking.

Long-term benefits: After over twenty-five years of research, the conclusions are that the High/Scope sample developed a framework for success in adult life that alleviated the negative affects of childhood poverty. A matched group did not. Female group members developed the interest and capacity to remain in school and graduate. Male group members showed greater social responsibility, and this included a distinct reduction in criminal and other anti-social behaviour.

Holistic Education

This approach tries to relate the educative process to the environment of the learner and teacher. The environment is not merely the classroom or even the local area, but the entire planet.

The basis for this educational ideal is the holistic view that all extant organisms on Earth are linked in one way or another, no matter how subtle, obvious and diverse. Consequently, in order for the human race to evolve without destroying its surroundings, it must understand and respect them. The best way of doing this is as part of the educative process, and the best time to start is as early as possible.

The goal of holistic education is to create a human society which is not only at peace within itself, but in harmony with its surroundings. Holism is intent on emphasising the human potential as positively as possible - developing creative, physical skills as well as mental, logical abilities.

Holistic education practices are guided by the belief that, in order to produce the society described above, human beings need to be far more fully developed than most are, and so rather than solely dictating facts for the mindless copying and memorisation by children, holistic education addresses the human need for justification and meaning - exploring not just What, When and How, but also Why.

Holistic educational practice does not lean on one particular curriculum or methodology but is a set of working assumptions including:
1. Education cultivates a critical awareness of the various contexts of people's lives - moral, cultural, ecological, economic, technological, political;
2. Human intelligence is expressed through diverse styles and capacities, all of which we need to respect;
3. Creative, intuitive, contextual and physical are all valid ways of knowing;
4. Learning is a life-long process;
5. Learning is both an inward discovery and a co-operative activity;
6. Learning is active, self-motivated, supportive and encouraging of the human spirit;
7. A holistic curriculum is interdisciplinary, integrating both community and global perspectives.

John Holt and Children as Natural Learners

John Holt (1923-85) established himself as a writer, educator, and lecturer of significance with the publication of his first book *How Children Fail.* He wrote ten books including other world best sellers such as *How Children Learn* and *The Underachieving School.* For John Holt, young children are 'natural' learners. They are like explorers or research scientists busily gathering information and making meaning out of the world. Most of this learning is not the result of teaching, but rather a constant and universal learning activity "as natural as breathing". If supported and encouraged, children will not only begin to make sense of their world, but will also acquire the attitudes and skills necessary for successful learning throughout their lives. But rigid, imposed systems introduced at some later stage in their education, could limit and then destroy the confidence-building processes that are initially established. This process of natural learning could be smothered by insensitive adult interference or 'unwanted teaching'.

His lecture tour to Europe in 1982 marked a change of focus in his writing. He was lecturing to audiences of people interested in home-based education as an alternative to schooling. He had decided to work with the few more positive parents involved in alternative small schools or home-based education, for it became clear to him that the great majority of boring, regimented schools were doing exactly what most people wanted them to do by teaching them that 'Life Is No Picnic' and getting them to learn to 'Shut Up And Do What You're Told'. The reasons for these bleak attitudes were not cruelty or mean-spiritedness *per se*, but fatalism. In their view, this was how the world was and that it would not change for the better.

His last two books, *Teach Your Own,* and *Learning All the Time,* emphasise and review the role of the more positive parents as educators. The vision John Holt had of a school is contained in these words:

"Why not then make schools into places in which children would be allowed, encouraged, and (if and when they asked) helped to explore and make sense of the world around them ... in the ways that most interested them?"

But the ways teachers needed to relate to students could not happen as long as schools were compulsory, because school attendance laws force teachers to do police work, preventing them from doing genuine teaching. He concluded that we needed to 'make schools less like schools'.

Home-based Education

In the UK, the USA and elsewhere an unusual, quiet revolution has been taking place in the form of educating children at home. At the same time as the fierce debates about mainstream education have been taking place concerning the National Curriculum, Testing, 'Back to Basics', Opting Out or Opting In, Local Management of Schools, etc., some families have quietly been getting on with a 'Do It Yourself' approach to education. In the USA over a million families are now 'home-schoolers' as they are known across the Atlantic. In the UK, 5,000 to 10,000 families are estimated to be operating home-based education. Thousands more are involved in Australia, New Zealand and Canada.

This phenomenon is most accurately described as home-based education because most families use the home as a springboard into community-based activities and investigations, replacing the 'day prison' model operated by most schools. People often find this quite hard to grasp, and wonder whether such children become socially inept. Yet it is soon clear that learning activities out in the community give children more social contacts, and more varied encounters than the restricted social life on offer in the majority of schools, as well as reducing the peer-dependency feature of adolescent experience.

People often try to generate generalisations and stereotypes about families educating the home-based way. The only ones that the evidence supports are that: **(a) they display considerable diversity in motive, methods and aims; and (b) they are remarkably successful in achieving their chosen aims**.

Schools often claim that if home-based education is to be tolerable, the families should learn how to do it from the 'professionals'. The evidence, however, is that schools often have more to learn from the flexibility of these families.

When schools were set up, we lived in an information-poor environment. Today we live in an information-rich environment. This is a major factor in contributing to the success of home-based education. Furthermore, schools were designed to produce rather rigid, conformist people on a production-line model. Today we need flexible, adaptable people the production-line approach does not produce. Until schools adapt, as a few have, home-based education will be the most generally effective and successful kind of education available.

(For further information, see *Education Otherwise* in the address list.)

Human Scale Education

This organisation is an educational charity set up in 1985 that exists to encourage 'human scale values' in education, in all schools and educational settings, large or small. It proposes that at the centre of the educational process should be the child, **not** the curriculum, **nor** the school, **nor** the requirements of the economy. Since children are individuals with different achievements and needs, this calls for a variety of schools and a diversity of learning experiences.

What these experiences need to have in common is the treatment of children as individuals with meaningful relationships with adults and that this can best take place in small groupings. What is needed:

- schools more like a family than a factory
- teachers who are both friends and mentors
- a curriculum tailored to the individual child
- parents involved as partners in the process of education

Human Scale Education supports:

Mini-schooling and other schemes that allow large schools to restructure into smaller units.

Small schools, urban and rural, and the encouragement of the setting-up of new ones.

Flexischooling, allowing parents to combine school with home-based education or community-based education.

These concepts are highlighted for their correspondence with the Human Scale Education ideal of small learning groups where learners and teachers get to know each other personally. This helps learners to learn at their own pace. Learners can also help each other to learn, as well as using the guidance of teachers and parents. Such an approach is a deliberate contrast with the depersonalised and alienating atmosphere which is currently commonplace within our schools. Teachers should teach children not subjects; a reduction in testing is a consequence. The approach advocated by HSE is holistic in the sense of stressing the development of the whole person and that this is a life-long enterprise.

Ivan Illich

The radical idea that we should abolish the existing school system was developed in his book *Deschooling Society* in 1971. It was part of Illich's general analysis of the detrimental effects on humans of the major institutions they had created, such as those for health, law, and mass communication. Schools hold a crucial place because they coerce people when young and gullible to accept the need for dependence on institutions to do things for them. After that they are deprived of the urge to grow up as independent, self-reliant, self-directing individuals.

The institutionalisation of society means that personal initiative, except that which is sanctioned by an institution, becomes regarded with suspicion. Ask any home-based educator and they will tell you the truth of this. Future actions are presented overwhelmingly in institutional terms - death means funeral directors, ill-health means doctors and hospitals, defending your rights mean lawyers, further learning means universities. The reason for school was that:

> *"School is necessary to produce the habits and expectations of the managed consumer society."*

Illich draws a distinction between **manipulative** and **convivial** institutions. The present manipulative version of school hijacks natural education:

> *"Education extracts the active ingredient of living a full, inquisitive life, calls it 'learning' and then attempts to improve this learning through bureaucratic administration of curriculum."*

If we could devise a learner-friendly, voluntary school instead of the manipulative one of compulsion and imposition, it would be acceptable within the definition of a convivial institution. Conviviality was seen as the freedom-based association of individuals in groups for comradeship and co-operation, infused with the joy of being alive.

The present dehumanised social structure that begins the cycle of its perpetuation through compulsory schooling was not seen by Illich as a cause for despair, but as a reason for radical thought and change. But he saw schools as changing more slowly than other institutions and may well be the last of the institutions to exchange compulsory manipulation for voluntary conviviality.

Learner-managed Learning

There is a long-standing tradition regarding autonomous learning, indeed it is as traditional as the idea of formal instruction and probably pre-dates it. Socrates was noted for the approach of advocating that a teacher enters into an individual dialogue with each pupil. Quintillian held that Roman education should follow similar principles:

> *"The skilled teacher, when a pupil is entrusted to his care, will first of all seek to discover his ability and natural disposition and will next observe how the mind of his pupil is to be handled ... for in this respect there is an unbelievable variety, and types of mind are no less numerous than types of body."*

Contemporary research supports Quintillian. Human beings, adults and children alike, differ from each other in learning styles. To date, over thirty such differences have been identified.

Ironically, we live in a society that expects you to manage your own life more and more, but takes over the management of learning of most people between the ages of five and sixteen, expecting attendance for a minimum of 15,000 hours to have the centrally-imposed National Curriculum transmitted to them in a 'tell them and test them' environment.

Some areas of learning are left for learners to manage for themselves such as learning car-driving, coping with sexual behaviour, and acquiring some skills of parenthood when children arrive.

Learners managing their own learning may, mistakenly, be assumed to be solo learners. This is neither a necessary condition nor a desirable one. What distinguishes learners managing their own learning is the motivation to choose to learn and to act upon that choice effectively. Whether that learning is carried out by working alone, or by working co-operatively in a group, or by deciding to submit to formal instruction, is not the issue. All these styles of learning can be harnessed in turn, if this is seen as appropriate, by the autonomous learners. What learners effectively managing their own learning do, is to follow the essential sequence of 'plan, do, review'.

(See also *Autonomous Education* and *High/Scope Perry Pre-school Project*.)

Libertarian Education (Lib. Ed.)

Lib. Ed. is the current name of a magazine and organisation that has been going for over twenty-five years. At first it was the magazine of the Libertarian Teachers' Association, but then, in order to recognise that learning was not and should not be teacher-orientated, changed to its present title. The group also publishes books, and both runs and contributes to conferences.

The magazine is written by the Libertarian Education Collective and is published three times a year. It provides a forum for the debate of radical theory and practice in education which is taken to be a lifelong process that is not confined to schools and colleges. Indeed, schools and colleges are often exposed as anti-educational and preventing the liberation of learning.

A main task of the group is to examine the way the UK society educates its members. Schools are seen as generally financed to deliver docile people to the factories, offices and retail organisations. Whenever more libertarian practices occur, Lib. Ed. writes about them. But since school is only one agent of conformity, Lib. Ed. looks at non-institutional learning, particularly at the mass media, from which we learn to have 'acceptable' attitudes and opinions.

The most difficult task is seen as suggesting ways of changing 'what is' into 'what might be'. To this end, a small but practical handbook *Freedom in Education* was produced in 1993.

The concept of freedom is central to the libertarian outlook. This requires that people are enabled to make choices and to make them in as free a way as possible. This means that the widest range of *genuine* alternatives is needed, with access to information from which people can make *informed* choices.

In the case of religion, for example, people would need to have access to information about Hinduism, Islam, Buddhism, Christianity, Taoism as well as non-religious life stances such as Marxism and Humanism before they can make an unconstrained choice as to which one is for them. This decision continues, in a situation of freedom, to be open to review and re-evaluation. The idea of compulsory worship and compulsory religious education predominately in one faith tradition is seen as mere indoctrination and the antithesis of freedom.

Margaret McMillan

Although born in America in 1860, Margaret McMillan spent most of her life in Britain. She was an ardent social and educational reformer, and her pioneering work in the nursery school she founded in Deptford, London, with her sister Rachel, has had a marked influence on the development of nursery education throughout the world. As a local politician, and with experience as a governess, she sat on School Boards in both Bradford and Deptford, regularly visiting schools over a period of 20 years. Here she found overwhelming evidence of child neglect; the result of poverty and appalling housing conditions. She was convinced that schools could not have much success when children were dirty, hungry and disease-ridden. In founding the pioneer open-air nursery school she intended to deal with the consequences of this poverty by improving the health of the children, providing them with the benefits of education, overcoming ignorance through work with their parents, but, most importantly, for school to be a place where children were loved and 'nurtured'.

'Nurture', to Margaret McMillan, involved concern for both physical growth and cognitive development. Having good food, fresh air, play space, baths and forming good habits of personal hygiene were important elements in nursery school life. Like Froebel, she believed in play as a vehicle for education, and wanted children to exercise responsible choice and discover for themselves through self-directed play. However, she appreciated that some structure and teaching would be necessary, such as appropriate teacher intervention to promote language development. She recognised the importance of the development of imagination and, unlike Montessori, believed that fairy stories were appropriate for young children. The dominant feature of the nursery was its garden; this was the real teaching area where the children could get fresh air and be close to nature. It was planned with space for play, flowers, trees, terraces, ponds, pools, fountains, animals and a kitchen garden. Shelters, to offer protection in inclement weather and house other facilities, were located around the garden. They had an opening south wall to let in sun and air. Each shelter had a 'family' group of 30+ children of mixed ages, usually two, three and four-year-olds (although parents were encouraged to keep their children there until they were seven), its own head teacher and four probationers. Overall, the shelters would house 200 to 400 children. They could be seen as an early form of 'mini-schooling'. The daily routine was flexible but provided a framework within which the children had opportunities to follow their own interests, use their initiative and co-operate with others, interspersed with meal-times, rest-times, washing routines, walks/visits and some planned activities.

Alice Miller: damage caused by authoritarian child-rearing

Polish by birth, Alice Miller has lived in Switzerland since 1946 where she taught and practised psychoanalysis. In her work she developed her theories about the destructive nature of orthodox child-rearing. In her first book *Prisoners of Childhood* (1981), Miller challenges the way child-rearing says that punishment and coercion are for the child's 'own good'. What is often known as 'good upbringing', Alice Miller sees as **the poisonous pedagogy**.

She opposes the view of Freud that violent impulses are the result of thwarted drives from within a person. Because Freud accepted the dictum that a person should 'honour their father and mother', he was blinded from seeing that the orthodox authoritarian child-rearing approach of parents was the cause of the problem. Drive theory acted as a smokesceen. It prevented people from confronting the many times in childhood that they had wanted warmth, or love, or understanding, from their parents, but got correction or 'discipline' instead.

Alice Miller's work enrages those who hold to the 'common sense' views about being tough with children. Good parents are supposedly those who make their children obedient and tolerate no dissent. Parents using this model cannot be expected to take kindly to an analysis that states that Hitler and all the leaders of the Third Reich were brought up this way, and that their sustained hate and oppression had its origins in such methods of upbringing. She describes the orthodox 'good parent' pattern as one of unrecognised and systematic child-abuse often fuelled by hidden desires for a kind of revenge for their own unhappy treatment as children. We will still continue to infect the next generation with the virus of "poisonous pedagogy" as long as we claim that this of upbringing is harmless. (From preface to *For Your Own Good.*)

Parents often have deceptive success with their coercive methods until their children reach puberty, when problems can suddenly erupt. Then we can all become victims of this mistreatment. She quotes the case of terrorists in Germany, who have been shown to have a similar upbringing to those of the leaders of the Third Reich:

> *"It is very difficult for people to believe the simple fact that every persecutor was once a victim. Yet it should be very obvious that someone who was allowed to feel free and strong from childhood does not have the need to humiliate another person."* (From *For Your Own Good*, page 249.)

Mini-schooling

Mini-schooling is a method of organising a large school into small sub-units. Each sub-unit, or mini-school, has its own small team of teachers, a defined student population of about 100 pupils, some autonomy over the use of time, some resources of its own and a base area in the school. Parents could attach themselves to this base to help out with the teaching, supervision, resources production, administration, maintenance, repair and decorating.

Mini-schooling is based on the idea that inside every large and inevitably, to some degree or other, impersonal school, are lots of small, personal, family-style schools waiting to be liberated. A large school becomes organised as a cluster of small learning communities or a federation of mini-schools.

From time to time, the pupils of a mini-school will visit other parts of the campus such as a Science Block, even though they have a science facility within their base area, to use special facilities. Another example is a Physical Education Block's facilities. Mini-school teachers will operate some of the time as specialist teachers in their chosen subject area with pupils other than their mini-school cohort.

Learners, teachers and parents all feel strongly identified with the mini-school with which they are involved. This has two particular benefits, the most significant is a fall in truancy rates among children and absenteeism among teachers, due to their enjoyment of time spent at the mini-school.

Because the mini-school is a common and unifying factor, the groups of teachers and parents are more inclined to see each other as people to work with rather than rivals to fight against. This is demonstrated by increased fund-raising successes. These indicate that if they know that they will see the full benefits, people will always be willing to contribute whatever they can towards their children's education.

The ideas and principles of mini-schooling were first implemented at Madeley Court School in Telford, Shropshire, under the direction of Philip Toogood. They are currently in operation at the Stantonbury Campus, Milton Keynes, Buckinghamshire.

(See entry on ***Stantonbury Campus*** and R. Meighan and P. Toogood, *Anatomy of Choice in Education*, chapter 2.)

Maria Montessori

Maria Montessori was born in Italy in 1869 where she became a doctor working with mentally and socially handicapped children. As a result she became interested in education. Her observations of young children led to the development of her methods, which are based on the idea that children learn from self-motivated activity within a highly structured environment. In her approach, prepared equipment and tasks were organised in a planned sequence which enabled children to work with a high level of independence. Preliminary observation of children established what they could already do. This was the starting point for their learning, enabling them to build on what they learnt and so achieve some success. She believed that young children travel through 'critical' periods in their development when various concepts and skills are more easily acquired. To this end, she prescribed prepared materials and real life experiences to facilitate the practice and development of specific skills during these receptive periods.

The planned environment advocated by Montessori provided a tranquil setting where children were protected from dominant adults. A teacher (directrice) in Montessori schools did not interact with children unless necessary, so ensuring that their concentration and independent activity were not interrupted. Montessori believed that adults can easily inhibit children's discoveries. The structured activities enabled children to learn regardless of the quality of the teacher. Self-discipline was also seen to be encouraged and learned mostly as a by-product through the absorption of the learners in their experiences.

Whilst Montessori believed that 'play is child's work', she only provided opportunities for play designed to promote the learning of specific skills and concepts, considering there to be no value in imaginative play. Fantasy was rejected as it did not present a true picture of reality. The rigid structures built in by Montessori did not allow for spontaneous, incidental learning, nor the opportunity to build on experiences children had outside school. They also did not recognise the individuality of children. She believed that set exercises to develop specific skills should precede creativity. The importance of talk and discussion in encouraging reflection was not recognised.

Montessori's view of young children as intrinsically motivated, independent, active learners, is acknowledged by those working with these young people today, although some of her methods are seen to be too limiting, not enabling full expression or development of wider aspects of learning.

National Coalition of Alternative Community Schools

This USA organisation is made up of groups, individuals and families with a concern for alternative education. Home-based education is known as 'home-schooling' in the USA and is therefore seen as part of the Coalition's activity.

'Alternative educational ideas' appears to be a growth area in the USA. Some industrial concerns in the USA are now supporting alternative approaches with grants designed to: *"enable those entrepreneurs and risk-takers in education to break up the institutional gridlock that has stifled innovation and creativity"* in the words of Nabisco's chairman Louis V. Gerstner. The Nabisco scheme is to be known as "Next Century Schools" and has an initial £5.3 million given to it to: *"find bold ideas and see if they work"*.

Citibank is another commercial concern with a similar view. One of the first beneficiaries of Citibank's grants will be the Coalition of Essential Schools. The object is to train teachers in the alternative approach of being 'coaches' rather than authoritarian instructors. The approach derives from the work of Dr. Theodore Sizer at Brown University and assumes that pupils are not vessels into which information is poured but active participants in deciding what and how they are to learn in the quest of learning how to think and use their minds.

NCACS in the USA thus finds itself in a situation where its ideas are changing from being seen as marginal to becoming potentially of central interest. As a non-profit making coalition of schools, groups, families and individuals, it is dedicated to providing the kind of personalities with the globally-orientated outlook needed to cope successfully with the society in which we live, as well as the desire to try to change it for the better. Although the hundreds of member schools and groups represent many different approaches to this challenge, there are certain basic ideas about which they agree.

The NCACS was set up to support and promote these educational experiments, to bring members together and give them strength, encouragement, new ideas and experiences and a sense of community in their common endeavours. It also serves as an advocate for alternative ideas in education by distributing information to the general public and to interested parties.

National Curriculum

The idea of a National Curriculum has little educational merit and a poor record.

1. Long experience around the world shows that the idea does not work.

The idea of a National Curriculum has been tried many times throughout the world. Hitler was very keen on the idea and it formed the backbone of the Nazi schooling system. Stalin was another enthusiast and adopted it for the USSR as well as the occupied countries such as Poland. The UK tried it in the 1800s and abandoned it as a total failure.

2. Putting the various National Curriculum offerings side by side exposes them as a mish-mash of adult hang-ups, country to country.

When you put them side by side marked variations occur. Sweden devotes about 30% of the time to the Social Sciences. The UK version devotes none. The USSR had no space for religion except as part of historical studies. The UK version has compulsory Christianity. Other countries have compulsory Islam, or whatever turns out to be the local belief system. In Poland the dictatorship of the 'Reds' requiring compulsory Marxism is now replaced there by the dictatorship of the 'Blacks' (the clergy) requiring Catholicism instead.

3. Children are prevented from doing more important types of learning.

There is always an opportunity cost. Whilst children are being compelled to learn whichever National Curriculum is imposed on them, they lose out on learning other things such as the skills of learner-managed learning or the skills of democratic co-operative learning. The hidden curriculum is a powerful factor, for children learn how to be taught and not how to learn, to avoid independent thinking and to become dependent on the authority of the minds of others.

4. The concept of a National Curriculum is immoral.

A National Curriculum can thus be seen as mind-rape. The victim is compelled into a place chosen by the adults. They are then subjected to the learning will of the adults and their agents by being forced to learn what the adults prescribe, whether they want to or not. The methods are dictated by the adults. The adults proclaim that the children need it and like it really. Children become passive and resigned after 15,000 hours of this treatment, and some are angry and resentful.

5. Nationalism, one of the most destructive ideas known, is celebrated, rather than Internationalism.

Each country puts its own national geography and history first and world studies a poor second, if it features at all. In literature, the UK requires the study of several plays, featuring dated ideas in elegant but ancient language. Music, art and science show the same patterns. Each National Curriculum is a jumble of topics selected according to various national prejudices.

Progressive Education

The term 'progressive education' is ambiguous. This ambiguity has been exploited by modern tabloid journalists and politicians to attack anything they happen to take a dislike to in schooling at any given time. The term 'progressive' has been used to refer to schools that have one or more of these features:

- fee-paying residential schools with a non-authoritarian philosophy,
- day-schools with a non-authoritarian approach,
- schools based on the idea of co-education rather than single-gender,
- an emphasis on the outdoor and rural life,
- schools emphasising the imagination via arts, music and crafts,
- education based on non-religious, naturalistic or secular life stances,
- informality, honesty, and frankness in relationships,
- democratic forms of organisation and/or learning,
- liberal individualism achieved through autonomous learning,
- a curriculum based on spiritualistic theories or mystical ideas,
- or a curriculum based on the psychology of the unconscious.

Some schools developed one selection from this list, others promoted other selections. In *Assessing Radical Education*, Nigel Wright sees the various roots of this miscellany of ideas in the work of Rousseau, Pestalozzi and Froebel, among others, leading up to the 'New Education' of the 1890s. This movement had two strands. One was the independent progressive schools catering for an almost exclusively middle class clientele. The other was a loosely defined progressive movement within the maintained sector. Wright notes that there were considerable differences between these two even though they were linked in the New Education Fellowship and its journal *New Era*.

John Shotton in *No Master High or Low* notes that there was confusion with the ideas of libertarianism and those of the progressive schools. Both claimed to be child-centred, but the various progressive schools usually turned out to be teacher-centred in the end: there was always a hidden authoritarian sting in the tail. At most, they were 'child-referenced' by trying to take some notice of what were assumed to be the needs and interests of children. These 'needs and interests' were more often deduced from psychology and psychiatry than from asking or consulting children, or even observing them without pre-conceived ideas. This helps explain why later observers of children like John Holt, Alice Miller and Bertrand Russell came to rather different conclusions about the education of children.

Regressive Education

In the UK and the USA, there has been a sustained attack, for about twenty years, on something labelled 'progressive education'. The attack was, at first, tentative, then more confident, and then strident. In the 1988 UK Education Act, and the various subsequent revisions, the attackers claimed victory. Yet the obscurity of the target makes the claim difficult to evaluate. There are two immediate problems. The first is, what is meant by progressive education, and the second, what is the nature of its replacement that is so superior. The opposite of progressive is regressive. So the mystery to be investigated is what is the nature of regressive education.

In *Theory and Practice of Regressive Education,* Roland Meighan shows how regressive education favours:
- tightly controlled learning rather than eclectic and spontaneous enquiry,
- a set curriculum imposed by adults is preferable to a self-directed one,
- the view that 'Life is no picnic, so school should be no picnic', so be fatalistic and endure it by getting toughened up,
- teaching being defined as formal instruction and authoritarian control,
- the idea that learning to work without pleasure in school is a necessary pre-requisite to coping with the pain, frustration and dullness of employment - that is if you get any,
- the production of rigid people who know their place in society are preferred to flexible, innovative people who might exercise their imagination in ways threatening to those who enjoy the privileges of the *status quo.*

One feature of the return of more regressive schooling has been the emphasis on subjects and the imposition of these on younger and younger children. Yet subjects have only a modest part to play in the scheme of things: they are only part, and a diminishing part at best, of the tool kit of knowledge. It may be that subject teachers have little or no future in education because all they know can be readily made available in books, interactive videos, computer programmes and distance teaching materials.

The conclusion is that the switch to regressive ideas in any schooling system is no more than an attempt to refine ancient machinery to try to make it more efficient in the pursuit of obsolete goals.

Carl Rogers: "No Curriculum Without Student Participation!"

The USA was founded on the principle that those who are affected by a decision have the right to partake in making the decision; hence the slogan 'No taxation without representation!' Carl Rogers believed that the democratic philosophy should be practised in classrooms with the approach of 'No curriculum without the learners having a say in the decision-making'. But in the common approach to schooling there was a fear of trusting students and sharing power with them. In the everyday life of institutions like schools, we are fearful of opting for the discipline of democracy, and resort to the inferior hierarchical order and authoritarian discipline instead.

Rogers saw that democracy and its values were actually **scorned and despised** in practice:

> *"Students do not participate in choosing the goals, the curriculum, or the manner of working. These things are chosen for the students. Students have no part in the choice of teaching personnel, nor any voice in educational policy. Likewise the teachers often have no choice in choosing their administrative officers... All this is in striking contrast to all the teaching about the virtues of democracy, the importance of the 'free world,' and the like. The political practices of the school stand in the most striking contrast to what is taught. While being taught that freedom and responsibility are the glorious features of our democracy, students are experiencing powerlessness, and as having almost no opportunity to exercise choice or carry responsibility."*

Carl Rogers wrote at times about 'non-directive teaching', elsewhere about 'person-centred teaching', and sometimes about 'teachers as facilitators'. Another analogy that is similar is that of teacher as 'learning coach'. Rogers saw that this had little appeal to teachers whose thrill was having a captive audience because students who are given the opportunity to learn using democratic methods and discipline, often forget to mention their teacher, but simply praise the psychological climate they experienced and the zest for learning that developed as a result. Therefore the rewards of being an excellent learning coach are different from those of being a brilliant instructor-teacher. Students remember the dazzling performers, but they remember only a little about what was taught. They remember much more about the learning that they had initiated, planned, executed and reviewed for themselves, but their teachers are apparently invisible.

Bertrand Russell

The general aim of education for Russell was to enable children to learn to think; it was not to get them to learn to think what their teachers think. This required giving them access to both the information and the mental habits necessary for forming independent judgements. In this cause, he proposed that, although the ideal system of education must be democratic, that is not instantly attainable due to the lack of experience of the young. The authoritarian approach, therefore, had a modest part to play, for, *"authority in education is to some extent unavoidable, and those who educate have to find a way of exercising authority in accordance with the spirit of liberty. Where authority is unavoidable, what is needed is* **reverence.** *... In education, with its codes of rules emanating from a government office, its large classes and fixed curriculum and overworked teachers, its determination to produce a dead level of glib mediocrity, the lack of reverence for the child is all but universal."*

The four major sources of authority, Russell proposed, are the State, Religion, the Teaching Profession and the Parents. Not one of these can be wholly trusted to care adequately for the interests of the children since each one has aims other than the welfare of the young. The State wants the child to serve the national interest, the national economy and to replicate the existing form of government. The rival religious groups want the child to serve for perpetuating their particular group and increasing the power of their priesthoods. The teaching profession, in a competitive world, too often regards the school in the same way that the State regards the nation, and wants the child to glorify the school. The parents want the child to be a credit to them not necessarily by being happy or virtuous, but by achieving the marks of worldly success and this is why *"parents are too often a drag upon the best educationalists."* The child itself, as an end in itself, as a separate human being with a claim to whatever happiness and well-being may be possible, does not come into these various external purposes, except very partially and inconsistently. Therefore, *"we must aim at having as little authority as possible, and to think out ways by which young people's natural desires and impulses can be utilised in education."*

He was, in the end, so unimpressed with what was on offer in most of the schools around him that he started his own school, Beacon Hill. Later, he expressed some satisfaction with the school and the education it provided for his own children as well as the others, but did conclude that he had overestimated how much children actually needed the company of other children and what they positively learned from their peer group.

Sands School

Sands is a day-school for boys and girls aged eleven to sixteen. The school is based on the belief that children who are trusted will become trustworthy, children who are respected will gain self-respect, and children who are cared for will learn to care for others.

Consequently, children share responsibility for the running of the school with the staff. The school is centred around the School Meeting which takes place every week. It is chaired by a pupil and pupils and teachers each have a vote. It has complete authority to make any decision at all about present or future arrangements and takes on the responsibilities usually regarded as the task of a headteacher.

Sands puts the well-being of the children before academic success for unless children feel valued and respected, their work is of little importance to them. Paradoxically, this results in many good academic performances and children at Sands often do better than they have previously done elsewhere.

All classes in Sands are small and teaching is based on the individual needs of each child. There is a fixed, but democratically devised timetable and students are expected to come to classes, but the final responsibility to attend is given to the pupil.

Sands employs no domestic staff, so all the cooking, cleaning and washing up is done by the pupils and teachers. Each day, lunch - for those who eat at the school - is prepared by a small group. The last fifteen minutes of each day are spent doing useful work such as cleaning, tidying and keeping the school in good order, and everyone has a job to do at this time. Decorating and minor repairs are also done by the pupils and teachers.

Three reasons are given for this policy. One is to save money so that fees can be kept low. The second is to give children experience in cooking, repairs and cleaning without the need for special and contrived lessons. The third is to avoid the unhealthy notion of there being a servant class to prepare your food and clear up after you. If the school really belongs to those using it, they must share the responsibility for keeping it presentable.

Schools Within Schools

'Schools within schools' is a form of mini-schooling. It is a method of organising a large school into small sub-units. Each sub-unit, or mini-school, has its own small team of teachers, a defined student population often of about 100 pupils, some autonomy over the use of time, some resources of its own and a base area in the school. Parents can attach themselves to this base to help out, assisting with the teaching, supervision, resources production, administration, maintenance, repair and decorating.

In 'schools within schools', however, the mini-schools are deliberately organised on different philosophies to provide a range of learning choices. There may be three types on offer, e.g. an authoritarian, a democratic and an autonomous mini-school. Other choices of philosophy and practice may be offered. Learners, parents, teachers are all able to choose the style of learning that suits them and to change their choices from time to time.

It is also possible to have mixed choices, for example to study sciences in a democratic mode, literature in an authoritarian mode, and language studies in an autonomous mode. All these studies would also be available in the other modes so that if studying science, say, in one mode is not so successful for an individual one year, they can try another mode in the next.

There is not only the gain of learning and teaching in a smaller and less impersonal unit, but a choice of learning styles as well. Thus the idea is taken one step further that inside every large, and inevitably, to some degree or other, impersonal school, are lots of small, personal, family-style schools waiting to be liberated. A large school becomes organised as a cluster of small learning communities operating a variety of learning styles and philosophies.

Teachers are also able to operate in different styles if they so desire, either by making a change from one year to the next, or by teaching two curriculum areas in two different mini-schools.

(See entry on *Mini-schooling*.)

The Small School at Hartland

The model adopted at this small school in 1982 was 'that of the family and not the factory'. Education is seen as a partnership between children, teachers, parents and the local community. In Denmark and the Netherlands, parents and local people often start a small school with government encouragement and financial support, but in the UK this does not happen. Therefore, the buildings had to be purchased by individual shareholders who are local people, parents and also concerned readers of *Resurgence*, who see this project as practical action to construct a better world. Charities, Trusts and individual donations have helped provide the running costs of salaries, books and equipment.

The Small School is trying to demonstrate that concern for the individual can be combined with a broad and relevant curriculum. The task is seen as not just saving a village school for the benefit of a few local families, but as trying to provide a model that could be the inspiration of similar ventures elsewhere. The Human Scale Education Movement was launched at the same time as the school to try to spread a message of hope that 'small can be beautiful' in an age of large and usually impersonal institutions that are seen as rather like factory farms, stifling creativity and churning out spiritually stunted people.

The school has grown from nine pupils to around thirty today in the age range 11 to 16. There are two full-time teachers, working on much-reduced salaries to help balance the budget, and a band of part-time teachers.

One visiting reporter, Val Hennessy, wrote for her magazine, that as the day progressed she was struck by the atmosphere of bustling diligence and friendly co-operation. She noticed that there were no disgruntled pupils, no shouting, none of the usual peer-group humiliations, none of the indignity of having to raise a hand and request a toilet break. For her, mutual trust and affection were the qualities that distinguished this school from others.

In his account of the school entitled *Inventing a School* the first head teacher, Colin Hodgetts, notes that key factors are outside the control of the school:

> *"We have had to adopt the national curriculum purely for financial reasons, even though we believe this initiative is doomed to failure ... Even the best schools have teachers marred by the ugly world and children already stamped with the defects that their parents condone by habit ..."*

Small Schools

Even smaller than small schools are homes, and as the evidence shows, home-based education is currently the most effective education on offer in the UK and the USA. This lends some credibility to the claim of the advocates of small schools that it is folly to destroy them without good reason, because they **operate like extended families.**

Next, there is the **efficiency** argument. If you have one bad school of one thousand pupils, you get a thousand person disaster. The same pupils in ten small schools would require them all to be bad to achieve the same disaster.

Thirdly, there is the **quality of relationships** - the propositon that small is more beautiful because it is more personal and human. Large schools run the constant risk of becoming impersonal because of the logistics of their organisation. Small schools can, of course, run a different risk - that of suffocation: smothering rather than mothering.

A further issue is that of **choice,** starting with parental choice. Those parents whose wealth allows them to choose tend to favour smallness. Those who are left often have largeness thrust upon them. Next, there is the matter of pupil choice. In a survey of pupils in schools in Britain, Canada and Australia, they were strongly in favour of small schools. Cohesiveness and satisfaction were seen as high and friction seen as low. School children really liked their small schools and enjoyed being there, because they provided positive learning environments. In the same survey, the teachers in these schools responded in the same favourable way, despite identifying a few possible drawbacks.

Small schools are an international experience for they exist in large countries and small, rich countries and poor. But although they are so common, they have both advocates and critics. Those in favour recommend their personal atmosphere and make claims for their role at the centre of a local community. Those against claim they are expensive, having high unit costs, and claim they can only offer a restricted curriculum.

In the UK, administrators with the latter view have been dominant and have forced many small school closures on often unwilling populations.

Stantonbury Campus

Stantonbury Campus is a school of over 2000 students for 12-18 year-olds in Milton Keynes, UK. Its intention is to combine the variety of resource provision that size can bring without becoming impersonal. The prospectus notes that the school: *"combines the flexibility and richness of resources that size brings, with an organisation that allows each student to feel secure and special, and that encourages individual challenge."*

Many large schools might claim the same intention but retain the impersonal large hierarchical structures that prevent it being achieved. Stantonbury has adopted the mini-schooling model, calling its sub-units 'halls', to increase its chances of achieving the stated aim. The school is divided up into five halls. One is for the post-16 year-olds and the other four operate as mini-schools, each composed of about 450 students working with 30 staff members.

Adults are also welcome to join in the daytime classes and study alongside the younger students, especially in the post-16 year-olds unit. Students are encouraged through a scheme of Campus Service to participate in the wider life of the campus and to gain experience of working in the community.

The curriculum is firmly authoritarian and based on the impostional style of the National Curriculum even though the school opted out to protect its independence of action. Through extra-curricular activities there is an attempt to soften this approach to some extent, especially in 'hall days' and 'activities weeks', as the prospectus states:

> *"All students on campus have a regular opportunity to choose from a number of academic, sporting or special interest options. These whole-day activities offer a varied collection of experiences which enhances and broadens the student's curriculum ... The last week of the school year is organised as an activities week."*

Adopting the mini-schooling model is the main radical feature of the school. For the rest, it operates as an attempted benign authoritarian institution with little attempt to adopt democratic forms of learning or organisation. Student involvement is concerned merely to *"provide formal and informal channels for views which are listened to and acted on"* and *"**allowing** (my emphasis) opportunities for choice in students' learning in the context of a broad and balanced curriculum."*

Rudolf Steiner and the Waldorf Schools

Steiner studied history, but later took to spiritualism and developed Anthroposophy, *"a path of knowledge which leads the spiritual in the human being to the spiritual in the universe"*. The twin concepts of reincarnation and karma are woven into his theory. According to the Steiner theory, a young child is still very close to heaven and childhood is a gradual process of incarnation into Earthly existence, not fully completed until the age of 21. For those who doubt the concepts of heaven, reincarnation and karma, however, all this is at the level of interesting, but not unappealing, speculation.

The educational approach that developed from Steiner's views has had considerable appeal to the non-materialistic. Education is to help the gradual emergence of the person and is to reflect the child's inner needs at each stage. Children should be allowed to grow slowly into the world. The focus of the kindergarten stage from three-and-a-half to six years - always part-time - is to foster play in an artistic and imaginative way. Children are encouraged to enter a world of fantasy and play through being surrounded by beautiful natural objects and in a secure creative environment. There are sympathetic links here with humanistic psychology and the idea of 'developmentally appropriate practice', as well as the studies on the upbringing of people who later were accorded the status of 'genius'. (In stark contrast is the work of Alice Miller on the upbringing of Hitler and the leaders of the Third Reich.)

Steiner proposed that the educational strategies changed with each stage. For the infant, education should be based on imitation; for childhood, artistic creativity with emphasis on kind authority; for adolescence, freedom and autonomy together with guidance and counselling. Waldorf Schools base their curriculum on this approach. All teaching methods should be 'warmed through' with feeling, for what is taught is of less significance than how it is taught. The Steiner curriculum is not seen as subject-based but child-based. Passing on information is seen as less important than exercising the 'soul faculties' of thinking, feeling, and willing. The emphasis for children and teachers alike is on fostering social values, courtesy, and consideration for others, and being truly happy and productive in their work. It is not difficult to see why those with a regressive approach in education have always oppressed and persecuted the Waldorf Schools for working to such ideas.

Structures of Learning

The common view that there is structured learning and unstructured learning turns out to be just loose thinking. *All* learning is structured but the issue is which particular *kind* of structure is being proposed.

The list includes learning structures that are:
eclectic
developmental
evolutionary and organic
holistic
pre-mapped
Another structures classification is past-orientated based on subjects; present-orientated, on integrated themes; and future-orientated, on learning skills.

Mostly when people talk of structured learning they mean **pre-mapped**. The structures have already been worked out in advance, as in the case of a subject or a selection of subjects, and they are then made available to the learners in some way. This represents a kind of ancestor-worship in assuming that a previous generation has 'solved' the problem of knowledge and all we need to do is replicate its solution. The pre-mapped structures, however, are full of errors that are constantly exposed as new knowledge is discovered.

The method of making the chosen knowledge available can be by one of the authoritarian methods of coercion and compulsion, or of persuasion, or of steering or of controlled interaction and dialogue. Other methods are the autonomous and the democratic.

Young children tend to use **eclectic** structures. They collect experiences, information, ideas, words in the manner of a squirrel collecting nuts and then make use of their store from time to time. They also make use of **holistic** structures, whereby the new pieces are fitted into a whole structure, however rudimentary and subject to revision it may be. **Evolutionary and organic** structures tend to be a reflection that the eclectic and holistic have a pattern that can, in retrospect, be identified.

Developmental structures are derived from observation of usual or common sequences from which it is assumed that the next generation will tend to follow the same general order but allowing for some individual differences in speed, learning style and pathways.

Sudbury Valley School, Massachusetts

The school operates as a living democracy and admits anyone who wishes to join, from age 4 to adult, paying no attention to previous school records and experiences. The school is committed to a democratic approach in a setting where people of all ages can feel comfortable, dignified and free to pursue their own interests. It is furnished more like a home than an institution with books around the walls of rooms rather than in a library. Most of the staff are part-time and have other careers outside the school. The school size varies from sixty to ninety.

There is no imposed timetable. Students have no schedules and are not assigned to any groups. Patterns of study emerge solely from the activity and decision of individuals or groups of students; any timetable is thus emergent, not pre-set. Staff members 'teach' in this setting mainly through conversations and responding to questions unless a more formal tutorial or course is requested. A staff member may offer a course and see if there are any takers. Age segregation is not practised and age mixing is the common experience in both formal and informal activities.

There are no institutional evaluations such as grades or reports. The high school diploma is awarded solely on the basis of a publicly defended thesis at a meeting open to all members of the school assembly which includes students, staff, parents, trustees and elected public members. A formal weekly School Meeting deals with the entire range of administrative, financial, staff appointments, rules, behaviour and building maintenance. There is also a Judicial Committee to deal with problems of order. The tuition fee is kept as low as possible.

A study of the results of such an education by Peter Gray and David Chanoff demonstrated that the Sudbury Valley students have had little difficulty in being admitted to universities or adjusting to the demands of their study programmes. They have been successful in a wide range of careers. Former students reported that they had appreciated being able to develop their own interests and that the school had fostered such traits as personal responsibility, initiative, curiosity, ability to communicate well with people regardless of status or age, and a continued appreciation and practice of democratic values in their everyday life. Many felt that the experience of being at the school had given them a head start in their careers compared with people coming from non-democratic schools.

Summerhill

Summerhill is, perhaps, the most famous 'free' school in the world. It was begun in Lyme Regis, UK in 1921 by A. S. Neill but has been at Leiston, Suffolk since 1927. The current director is Neill's daughter Zoe Redhead, who stays close to the philosophy articulated by her father. It is an international residential school occupying a Victorian mansion and its grounds. There are about fifty children between the ages of four and sixteen from various countries including UK, USA, France, Japan and Germany. The school is financed through fees and some donations, but has no state funding or other outside help. Matters of health, safety and finance are seen as the prior, though not sole, concern of the Director.

The organisation of the school is democratic: all the members of the Summerhill community meet to make decisions about the day-to-day running of the school. The Meeting deals with general rules and organisation and the Tribunal deals with any anti-social behaviour. These are weekly meetings and the Ombudsmen are volunteer arbitrators from amongst the children who change one a fortnight and who try to settle any minor problems that arise. There are also various committees that run social and other events. Within this democratic framework, students are free to decide how they spend their time as no lessons are compulsory.

Summerhill is seen both as a 'free' school and a libertarian school because of its stress on the freedom of the members to choose. Thus they can choose how to spend their time by going along to lessons or not. Incidental learning is valued. Albert Lamb, a former pupil who later became a teacher at Summerhill, wrote:

"I believe a free school is a place where, as long as children are not breaking the community's laws or hurting anyone else they are free to do as they please. Lessons should be available but not compulsory. Social control should be administered democratically through a system of self-government. The purpose of such schools is to turn out emotionally strong people who can go on to achieve whatever goal they set for themselves ... Part of the trouble is that people think freedom is easy. It is not. It is a complex thing needing understanding of the adult/child relationship in order to get it right. It also needs democratic structures that can help reduce the wear and tear on everyone concerned."

Uniforms

In USA and UK, school uniforms are back in fashion, for unexpected reasons:

1. Uniforms will protect you from market forces.
Parents complain that they cannot cope with the pressure to buy particular footwear and clothing widely advertised and designed for the market of young people. If the school will only adopt and enforce a school uniform, parents and children will be protected from the unrelenting market forces. My friend who heads a Midlands grammar school, confirmed that this plea had now replaced any arguments about sparing the embarrassment of the poorer children, the need for egalitarianism, the desirability of a corporate image discipline or communal identity. The respite from market forces is only temporary, since on leaving school the market forces will then be unleashed on the young.

2. Uniforms will protect you from the influence of street gangs.
Thus a new state law in California to permit school uniforms is intended to control the influence of gang styles which usually involve baggy shorts and a baseball cap worn backwards, in blue if you belong to one gang or red if you belong to the rival gang. Gang members wear strictly enforced colour schemes and punish gang members who infringe the rules. Children have been killed for gang dress misdemeanours. They helped swell the ranks of the 50,000 children killed by guns within the USA 1979 - 1991. The replacement school-gang uniform of dark trousers or skirts with lighter tops is thought to require less drastic enforcement.

3. Uniforms will protect you from guns and knives.
In USA, school uniforms are now available in bullet-proof and knife-proof versions. Violent death at the hands of other children is increasing. In Chicago alone, 60 children were murdered in 1993, many of them in school buildings and playgrounds. The James Bulger murder by children in UK stirred up strong feelings. In USA such incidents have become all too common. The vast majority of them are drugs- and gang-related, and an estimated 270,000 students carry a gun to school each day.

"Nobody believes it can happen here," I told my USA visitor. *"That's what we thought only a few years back,"* he replied. He went on to propose that if children are more selfish, nasty and violent, it is because society has become more selfish, nasty and violent; the youth unemployment and the drug scene are both growing rapidly in UK as they did in USA, and the rest will follow.

Uppattinas Educational Resource Centre, Glenmoore, PA, USA

The re-creation of the Uppattinas school came after a long and painful struggle when the members faced up to the fact that there just were not enough students who could pay sufficient tuition fees, or families who could work hard enough to make up for that the shortfall in finances, to sustain the needs of the physical plant, or the teachers required for maintaining it as a 'school'. But it was possible to sustain the physical plant and preserve the integrity of its original commitment to open education through establishing it as a Learning Resource Centre which could be a 'school' or 'un-school', depending on the needs of the members. The director of the centre, Sandy Hurst, explained:

"That was a direction in which I was headed personally and something into which I could put the energy needed for organisation and direction. This could once again be a place to which people came who truly wanted to learn and to share what they had learned."

Based on the idea that we learn everywhere so school is everywhere, then the new Uppattinas is a part of that learning and is still a school. It continues to be a centre for people who want to make contact with others, for learning and sharing, for doing group projects or individual projects, for meeting and for growing together. It is not circumscribed by age limits or time limits. Everyone is welcome and the facility is open to community members as and when they need it. Programmes are limited only by the interests and needs of those involved.

The centre of activities has become families who educate their children at home and use the centre to augment their programmes of study, and students who come to the centre for classes. Workshops and special activities like music and drama are arranged as they are needed by the community. Facilities are available for group meetings large and small, and for many kinds of activities for people of all ages. Workshops have been organised ranging from music improvisation to American Indian survival skills; projects on a variety of environmental concerns; and classes spanning American Literature to First Aid. A list of teachers available to those who need them is kept up-to-date.

The work of the centre is growing and developing and its members currently see it as, *"a doing centre for all ages, a repository for tools for doing things, a repository for records of things done, a place for sharing, a source of helpers, a centre for people from all cultures, a source for participant controlled learning, a centre for all who believe in life-long learning."*

Willington Flexi-college

Willington Village College is a small secondary school, comprising two learning groups of students, one of 11 to 14 year olds and the other of 14 to 16 year olds. Based in South Derbyshire, the College is the first of a planned cluster of small tutor groups operating the Flexi-college system of co-operative education.

Flexi-college is defined as a flexible college in the community. It aims to avoid setting learning apart from the community of business, or the family, or everyday life, but will be set in the middle, supporting and reinforcing the interests of the individual and society in a way that institutions set apart find it very difficult to do. The intention is to abolish the duality of education and living. Parents are closely involved in the running of the flexi-college as part of this philosophy.

Richard Terry writes from his experience as a flexi-college tutor:

"As a co-operative learning group we are constantly reviewing, criticising, and revising our methods, times, and practice. However, we strive to maintain a core structure which underpins everything we do, based on the assumption that it is desirable that all students learn to take responsibility for their own learning. This does not happen overnight, nor with the greatest of ease; on the contrary, it requires hard, often stressful, work. Also required are: a readiness to accept and adapt to changes; and, above all, the careful nurturing of a set of relationships based on mutual respect and trust."

Students learn from small group living, work experience, community service, vocational training and academic courses. They can prepare for a wide range of examinations at GCSE level as well as the new National Vocational Qualifications. A democratic approach to living and learning is being developed.

Flexi-college is an initiative pioneered by Philip Toogood, building on his earlier ventures in developing mini-schooling in a large comprehensive school, and evolving from his work as head of the Dame Catherine's School.

(see entry on *Dame Catherine's School*)

The Woodcraft Folk

This national organisation operates as an alternative to the Scouts and Guides. It broke away from the Scouts in the 1920s in reaction to what was seen as the militaristic and sexist style of that organisation. The Woodcraft Folk was assisted from the start by the Co-op and has been associated with the Co-operative Movement ever since.

There are over 700 groups throughout Britain. Groups welcome boys and girls of the following ages:
> Elfins 6-9 years, Pioneers 10-12 years, Venturers 13-15 years,
> and District Fellows 16-20 years.

Members experience an active and varied programme designed to meet the specific needs of each age group.

The Woodcraft Folk seek to educate its members for citizenship and community service in adult life. The programmes aim to achieve:

- the learning of co-operation and democracy,
- the appreciation of the need to help others,
- the necessity of international understanding.

Indoor activities include weekly group meetings for games, craftwork, festivals, folk-singing, folk-dancing, dramatics, film shows, and discussions.

Outdoor activities include weekend and summer camps, youth hostelling, visits, rallies, hikes, and training schools.

International activities are encouraged through the contacts the Woodcraft Folk have with similar organisations all over Europe. It organises and attends large and small international events lasting from two to four weeks. Group exchange visits are encouraged and members act as hosts at local camps and offer hospitality in their homes. Many firm and lasting friendships are made as members strive to live up to their motto of:

"Span the World with friendship."

World-wide Education Service (WES)

WES is part of the education charity PNEU (Parents' National Educational Union) founded by Charlotte Mason in the 1880s. WES Home-Schools have been operating throughout the world for over 100 years. The one-to-one teaching situation of a parent and a child is one of the reasons why the standards achieved are high.

The WES Home-School system involves the creation of a school in the home. Parents rarely have previous experience of teaching and none is expected. They are provided with the necessary guidance and materials to teach their children themselves.

A year's programme is provided with detailed advice to the parents on 'how' as well as 'what' to teach their child. All books required are provided by WES. The curriculum shadows that of schools in Britain and transfer into British schools presents little difficulty, except the common experience of WES pupils finding they are ahead in many cases.

Families are allotted a tutor who they usually meet at the outset and at other times as desired. The tutor provides help and guidance by correspondence and monitors the progress through scrutinising termly samples of work and providing feedback. The Home-School is flexible and can be tailored to the circumstances of a particular family, e.g. the school year can be started and spread out as the family thinks fit.

WES has been adopted by various companies as a solution to their problems of posting staff overseas and the courses have the approval of the Department for Education, the British Council and other official bodies. Thus ex-patriate families have been the major clients.

In the last few years, however, WES has recognised the rapid growth of home-based education in the UK and has developed a flexible range of services to cater for this development.

Addresses

Advisory Centre for Education (ACE), 1B Aberdeen Studios, 22-24 Highbury Grove, London N5 2EA.

Children's Legal Centre, 20 Compton Terrace, London N1 2UN.

Community Education Development Centre, Lyng Hall, Blackberry Lane, Coventry CV2 3JS.

Dame Catherine's School, Rose Lane, Ticknall, Derbyshire DE73 1JW.

Democratic Education: Institute for Democratic Education UK Office, c/o Dr. Clive Harber, School of Education, University of Birmingham B15 2TT.

Dyslexia Initiative, Centre for Personalised Education, The Burntlands, Upper Rochford, Tenbury Wells, WR15 8SH.

Education Otherwise, P.O. Box 120, Leamington Spa, Warwickshire, CV32 7ER.

Education Now, 113 Arundel Drive, Bramcote Hills, Nottingham NG9 3FQ.

Green Teacher, Machynlleth, Wales, SY20 8DN.

Holistic Education Network, 81 Guiness Court, Mansell Street, Aldgate, London E1 8AE.

Human Scale Education, 96 Carlincott, near Bath BA2 8AW.

Libertarian Education Collective, Phoenix House, 170 Wells Road, Bristol BS4 2AG.

Sands School, 48 East Street, Ashburton, Devon TQ13 7AX.

The Small School, Fore Street, Hartland, Bideford, Devon.

Steiner Schools, Kidbrooke Grove, Forest Row, East Sussex RH18 5JB.

Worldwide Education Service, 35 Belgrave Square, London SW1X 8QB.

The Woodcraft Folk, 13 Ritherdon Road, London SW17.

Index

Selected References.

Dewey, J., (1956) *The Child and the Curriculum* Chicago: Univ. Chicago Press.

Harber, C., and Meighan, R., (1988) *The Democratic School* Ticknall: Education Now Books.

Hodgetts, C., (1991) *Inventing a School: The Small School* Hartland: Resurgence.

Illich, I., (1971) *Deschooling Society* London: Calder and Boyars.

Meighan, R., (1988) *Flexi-schooling* Ticknall: Education Now Books.

Meighan, R., ed. (1992) *Learning from Home-based Education* Ticknall: Education Now Books.

Meighan, R., (1994) *Theory and Practice of Regressive Education* Nottingham: Educational Heretics Press.

Meighan, R., (1995) *John Holt: Personalised Education and the Reconstruction of Schooling* Ticknall: Education Now Books.

Meighan, R., and Toogood, P., (1991) *Anatomy of Choice in Education* Ticknall: Education Now Books.

Miller, A., (1987) *For Your Own Good: Hidden Cruelty in Child-rearing and the Roots of Violence*, Virago: London.

Neill, A. S., (1962) *Summerhill* London: Gollancz.

Shotton, J., (1993) *No Master High or Low: Libertarian Education and Schooling 1890-1990* Bristol: Libertarian Education.

Shute, C., (1994) *Compulsory Schooling Disease* Nottingham: Educational Heretics Press.

Wright, N., (1989) *Assessing Radical Education* Milton Keynes: Open University Press.

(for a more extensive list see p.276 of Shotton, J., *No Master High or Low*)

THE FREETHINKERS' GUIDE TO THE EDUCATIONAL UNIVERSE

A Selection of Quotations on Education
compiled by Roland Meighan

James Hemming comments: *"Where this volume of quotations makes such an impact is in showing what a powerful consensus exists among thinkers of all ages on what education is really about: the awakening of young minds to the challenge of being alive, involved and responsible."*

Matthew Parris, the Times columnist, has been kind enough to say about this book: *"It's a brilliant collection. ... Good luck with it."*

Lord Judd writes: *"It's super! And sobering."*

This source book has multiple uses. It can be used for discussions and also to provide illustrative material for lectures, lessons and seminars. Students will also find the contents useful in the preparation of their essays on educational and related themes. The book is produced in hardback for use as a library or classroom reference book, or as a coffee-table source book. Most of the quotations from the earlier and shorter paperback version, which came out under a different title and sold out rapidly, have been retained and augmented with additional ones.

The quotations are produced in large bold type to allow direct transfer to overhead projector transparencies or into lecture or seminar handouts. One respondent enthused that since he works with visually handicapped students, he will find this feature of the book very useful.

ISBN 0-9518022-4-0

Price: £12-50 (postage and packing inclusive) and available in hardback only.

Available direct from:
Educational Heretics Press, 113 Arundel Drive, Bramcote Hills, Nottingham NG9 3FQ

COMPULSORY SCHOOLING DISEASE

After twenty-five years as a modern languages teacher, Chris Shute, in his first book, presents his misgivings about schooling:

"I agreed to write this book because, after twenty-five years of school-teaching I became convinced that I was engaged in a form of microcosmic fascism. I intend to show in this book that schooling is, indeed, an activity which has aspects in common with fascism. That is not to say that teachers mean it to be so, or that they are conscious of the evil in which they are involved. Even fascism in its early phases attracted some reasonable, high-minded people who believed that the world could be changed for the better merely by the use of a little force and rigour in the right place."

"Perhaps their (my fellow teachers) true motivation was summed up for me by a lady colleague of mine some years ago. I had been talking to her about the grey, strained expressions I saw on the faces of my pupils as they went about the school. I suggested that it might be something to do with their feeling that they were not being educated so much as sentenced to hard labour for the crime of being children. She thought for a moment, and said in a grim voice: "I went through it. I see no reason why my child should escape.""

"I cannot bring myself to see education as she (my colleague) saw it, a life-long campaign against spontaneity, liveliness, and the natural energy of youth. Neither can I accept that the anger and frustration I saw in those children, which I now recognise as the same anger that slaves and occupied people feel, serves any good purpose in education."

"Home-based education or home-schooling is not discussed. This is not because I do not take it seriously as a method of educating children. In fact, I believe it is currently the best way to educate most children. But I hope that one day soon it will be possible for children to use schools as they should be used, as places where any person who happens to need help with their studies can go and receive it. Until that time, I must confine myself to commenting on schools as they are now, and challenging us to consider whether their regime contributes to enslaving the minds of children rather than setting them free."

ISBN 0-9518022-1-6   Price £6-00   (p.&p. included)

Educational Heretics Press, 113 Arundel Drive, Bramcote Hills, Nottingham NG9 3FQ

ALICE MILLER; THE UNKIND SOCIETY, PARENTING, AND SCHOOLING

by Chris Shute

Alice Miller wrote several books in which she revealed how, after many years as a practitioner of traditional psychoanalysis, she came to believe that she had discovered the true origin of the vein of ferocity which runs through human relationships everywhere. Her training had led her to assume that people become neurotic because they had not succeeded in resolving the conflicts with their parents resulting from their innate drives. It was only when she was able to detach herself from the Freudian presuppositions on which psychoanalysis is based and establish communication with her own childhood feelings that she realised a simple but revolutionary truth: people are not emotionally distorted by their unresolved Oedipus Complex, or by some complex mismanagement of their imperious, inescapable drives. Instead, it is the unrecognised cruelty of their parents, masquerading as 'firm discipline' and 'responsible control', which injects slow-acting poison into their lives.

Young children are utterly helpless. If their parents respect and respond to their inarticulate attempts at communication with the outside world by all the means in their power, well and good. But if they have learned from their own background and culture to believe that children are wicked and in need of repression, they will crush, 'for their own good', all their innocent attempts to act independently , leaving them angry, frightened, and frustrated. They will have learned that it is dangerous to resist the god-like power of their parents, and in the end they will solve their problems by the only means available to them: **they will forget the tragedy of their early years and grow up into a faithful imitators of those who oppressed them.**

Alice Miller's books convinced me that bad education (most modern education is bad because it is cruel and insensitive), painful child-rearing and political tyranny all have the same source: the well-nigh universal delusion that children do not feel, and that it doesn't matter what adults do to them. I want to encourage as many people as possible to read what Dr. Miller has written and to apply it seriously to their own thinking.

ISBN   1-9518022-5-9   Price £6-00 (p.& p. included)

Educational Heretics Press, 113 Arundel Drive, Bramcote Hills, Nottingham NG9 3FQ